# Last Stands

*A Journey Through*
*North America's Vanishing*
*Ancient Rainforests*

Larry Pynn

Oregon State University Press
Corvallis

The paper in this book meets the guidelines for permanence
and durability of the Committee on Production Guidelines
for Book Longevity of the Council on Library Resources and
the minimum requirements of the American National
Standard for Permanence of Paper for Printed Library
Materials Z39.48-1984.

Library of Congress Cataloguing-in-Publication
CIP data available from the Library of Congress

ISBN 0-87071-027-3

Oregon State University Press
101 Waldo Hall
Corvallis OR 97331-6407
541-737-3166 / fax 541-737-3170
http://osu.orst.edu/dept/press

*To my sisters,*
*Kathy and Isabel, and brother, Brian:*
*supportive branches of my own family tree.*

# Contents

# Foreword

THE TEMPERATE rainforest may appear as a seamless vertical land-scape extending down the Pacific Coast of North America, but it is actually rudely interrupted at the 49th parallel by the border post of culture. Any journalist writing about this shared territory for audiences on both sides of the border must deal with that reality right from the outset. The United States stubbornly remains the last major nation to adhere to the old system of Imperial measurement, while Canada, a quarter century after embarking down the road to official metrification, still keeps a foot — 30 centimetres, if you prefer — firmly planted in each system of measurement. Canadians may know that 30 degrees is a heat wave or that 100 kilometres is an easy hour's drive on the freeway. But we still think of our weight in pounds, our height in feet and inches, our land in acres. So, at the risk of being viewed as inconsistent, this book attempts to take into account these realities of everyday life, using metric or Imperial measurements where it makes the most practical sense and stands to be most easily understood by the greater audience. To ease the transition, however, it might be helpful to observe that a yard is a shade more than a metre, a mile is half again as long as a kilometre, a kilogram is just over two pounds, almost four litres fit into a U.S. gallon, and an inch is 2.5 centimetres.

Wildlife researchers on both sides of the border are harmonized to the metric system, and to these individuals I offer special thanks. During a quarter-century of journalism, some of my most unforgettable moments have occurred in the company of wildlife researchers. I fully realize their work can be tedious, involving long hours of repetitive note-taking under difficult and occasionally dangerous field conditions. But as the journalist who sticks around for only a few days, creams off the best of the research, then moves on to another adventure, I am much better acquainted with the rewards of the job. For example, the privilege of getting to know a grizzly bear on a first-name basis; of finding a marbled murrelet nest on a pocket of old-growth moss high in the upper canopy; of wrapping a radio-collar around the warm, furry neck of a wolverine as it sleeps in your arms; of poking your head inside a rainforest limestone cave that is a portal to a past civilization. If I have been an intrusion or a pain during these scientific forays, I apologize. I suspect, however, that the most trying part of a researcher's work is not necessarily the field work or the unravelling of obscure biology, but achieving public and political support for one's findings. If I have assisted in that process, I've paid my dues.

Of course, scientists are only part of the underpinning of this book. The generosity of the public in opening up their lives, telling me their personal perspectives of the rainforest is also much appreciated. I do not enjoy bear hunting, but I give credit to the two hunters who had the guts to take me along with them to hear their story. And as difficult as it is to watch a 500-year-old tree collapse under the bite of a chainsaw, I am indebted to the loggers for letting me in on the process.

Many of these people — be they scientists or lay citizens — are named in this book. But others are not and deserve recognition. Thanks to Kurt Grimm, an assistant professor of earth and ocean sciences at the University of British Columbia, who showed me the big picture, but was always there to answer the little questions, too. Ken Drushka surely remains the single greatest authority on the history of industrial logging on the coast. George Barton shared his vast knowledge of the unique and wonderful properties of western red cedar. Through interviews and their writings, Jim Pojar and Andy MacKinnon offered extensive background information on coastal plants. Fisheries biologist David Anderson helped to explain the fisheries resources of Redwood National Park. And Wind River Canopy Crane in southern Washington allowed me the unique opportunity of viewing a rainforest from the top down.

Parts of this book have appeared in the *Vancouver Sun*, where I have worked full-time as a news reporter since 1977, as well as *Beautiful British Columbia* magazine, *Canadian Geographic*, and the *Georgia Straight*. I especially appreciate the *Sun*'s supportive editors, John Drabble and Graham Rockingham, for giving me time to write this book when they required my resources in the newsroom. *Beautiful British Columbia* editor Bryan McGill deserves special mention for continually sending me to the province's most spectacular natural places. Miguel Moya, my friend and colleague, consistently put time aside to help me as needed. And my travel partner, Janie Tyerman, an excellent photographer and dedicated sun worshipper, accompanied me to some of the wettest places on the continent for a book that contains no pictures. May our experiences shine on long after the rain has stopped.

# Last Stands

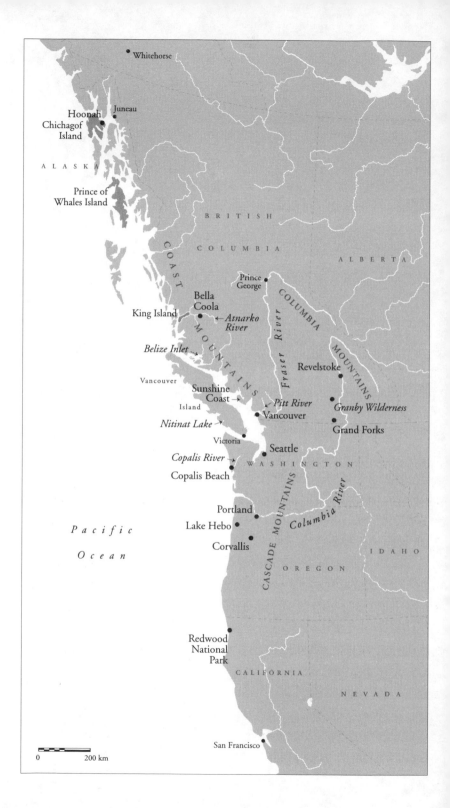

Whitehorse

Hoonah
Chichagof
Island

Juneau

ALASKA

Prince of
Whales Island

BRITISH

COLUMBIA

ALBERTA

COAST

Prince
George

Bella
Coola

King Island

←Atnarko
River

COLUMBIA

Fraser River

MOUNTAINS

Belize Inlet →

Revelstoke

MOUNTAINS

Vancouver

Sunshine
Coast →

Island

Pitt River

Granby Wilderness

Vancouver

Nitinat Lake →

Grand Forks

Victoria

Seattle

Copalis River →

WASHINGTON

Copalis Beach

Portland

CASCADE MOUNTAINS

Columbia River

Pacific

Lake Hebo

Corvallis

IDAHO

Ocean

OREGON

Redwood
National
Park

CALIFORNIA

NEVADA

San Francisco

0       200 km

# Introduction

A QUARTER OF a century ago I viewed the rainforest not as a magnificent, complex landscape, but as sawed-up chunks and slabs of western red cedar produced by the mill where I worked in suburban Vancouver.

Sometimes I labored on the green chain, handing off heavy blocks of ancient wood to a sawyer to be hewn into commercial shakes and shingles for residential construction. On other occasions I stacked bundles onto semi-trailer trucks to be shipped to markets throughout the Pacific Northwest. Once I even tried an unsuccessful stint on the water, using a pike pole to haul raw logs up to a cutoff saw, a career mercifully sliced short when I fell into the Fraser River halfway through my first shift.

But as a teenager growing up in the early 1970s, most of my

weekend work occurred on Sundays, alone, when the mill was closed. For eight hours and without any breathing protection I endured toxic clouds of ash and obscenely high temperatures while cleaning crusty, smoldering mounds of rendered wood waste — rainforest meltdown — inside the guts of a beehive burner. Like a good soldier of fortune (a union wage of $4.45 an hour allowed me an outboard ski boat, 350 cc Yamaha motorcycle, and '65 Chevy), I dutifully followed my supervisor's orders and hauled the ash by wheelbarrow to the shores of the Fraser River. There I paused for a moment to ensure no authorities were in view, then dumped it down the riverbank and returned to the hive for more. Over and over, weekend after weekend. I now rationalize my actions by arguing that I was young and it was a different era, a time when environmentalism was still finding its wobbly legs. But to this day I regret what I did. That I mention it here is not so much an act of catharsis as an indicator of the starting point for my unlikely journey to environmental writing.

Not that the journey ever really ends, of course; one's thoughts on logging and conservation continue to evolve with every new foray into the bush. I have covered more than 300,000 kilometres in twelve years in my two-wheel-drive Toyota pickup truck — ole Bessie — much of that bouncing around the labyrinth of logging roads that lace the industrial sole of British Columbia. I have seen much and talked to many people during that time. In doing so, I have inevitably forged certain sympathies for the plight of the Pacific temperate rainforest, a misunderstood place that suffers from the obscenity of polarized debate.

It occurred to me three years ago, when I first waded into the waters of this project, that there was much to be said about the rainforest that could not be told in the confines of a daily newspaper or a photo-filled coffee-table book. I also concluded that to tell the broader story, to journey first-hand through this unexplored void, I must adopt an approach as diverse and unconventional as the rain-forest itself. I chose to travel along the 4,000 kilometres of western North America, from northern California to southeastern Alaska, seeking out as many perspectives, as many parts of the whole, as pos-sible, in order to paint a more complete portrait of the temperate rainforest. I would ride along with black-bear hunters; stand with new-age loggers as they toiled beneath the lethal, churning blades of a heli-logging operation; glimpse the precarious reality behind the wolverine's legendary ferocity; travel old logging roads that are bleed-ing away the redwoods; explore the mysterious life-preserving resins that make red cedar the cultural lifeblood of the rainforest; go under-ground in search of the rainforest's oldest human bones; and fulfill my own destiny in a week-long solo hike through an uncharted wilder-ness. All seemingly disparate experiences, yet each representative of an ecological thread that binds or, in some cases, tears apart the rain-forest.

Along the way I spent considerable time with scientists, whose voices are too often silenced by the din of political rhetoric. It is not that I dismiss the opinions of people who lack a science degree. Far from it. I do not have one myself and would like to think I have some-thing to say on the subject. It is just that scientists are at the forefront of our knowledge of the rainforest.

Certain matters of natural history should be explained right from the outset. The first and most obvious issue is the definition of a tem-perate rainforest. Anyone caught camping unprepared during a pro-longed rainstorm on the Pacific coast has a very personal definition, and I am no different. As a neophyte outdoorsman fifteen years ago, I went camping in the upper reaches of Lynn Creek in the Coast Mountains immediately north of Vancouver. The spring had been typically wet, the rainforest dripping with humidity. Unable to even light a newspaper to kickstart a campfire, I was forced to subsist on raw rations, including boil-in-a-bag Chinese food, while the weather ranged from pelting rain to wet, driving snow. Ultimately, I realized, the rainforest is a state of mind.

Ecologists understand rainforests as consisting largely of vegetation that thrives in wet conditions, which, on the West Coast, is loosely understood to be at least 200 centimetres or eighty inches of precipitation annually. On the Pacific coast of my home province of British Columbia, that primarily covers two biogeoclimatic zones where moist temperate air trapped by the coastal mountains creates the rain that nourishes the forests: the coastal western hemlock zone, including the Coast Range and the west side of both Vancouver Island and the Cascade Mountains; and the mountain hemlock zone, located at higher elevations along the coast. A third temperate rainforest is the Interior cedar-hemlock zone, found in pockets of mountainous terrain several hours' drive east of the Pacific Ocean.

Of course, mean figures do not accurately reflect the sort of extreme lashing a rainforest is capable of dishing out. Henderson Lake, on the west coast of Vancouver Island, in 1997 set a Canadian rainfall record of nine metres for the year, 5.5 times the amount recorded at Vancouver International Airport. The lone occupants of this place are Bruce and Joanne Hepburn, operators of a salmon hatchery at the end of the boomerang-shaped lake that is surrounded by mountains and exposed to the the full brunt of the Pacific winds. Their clothes closet is loaded with rubber boots and raingear, but not a single umbrella. "You see people in Vancouver with umbrellas, walking along with frowns on their faces when it rains," Bruce told me when I paid a visit by chartered float plane. "But out here, where you know it's going to rain, you get used to it, you get around it."

The temperate rainforests of North America's Pacific coast are also distinguished by their preponderance of coniferous evergreens — softwood species such as western red cedar, western hemlock, Douglas fir, Sitka spruce — growing year-round in mild, wet conditions. These softwoods make for a landscape that may lack the East Coast's spectacular displays of autumn colors, but more than compensates with an emerald broadloom that remains lush and vibrant throughout the year. The most remarkable of these coastal temperate rainforests feature the last stands of ancient old growth, trees as broad as buses and tall as apartment buildings; trees at least 250 years old but capable of living well beyond 1,000 years.

Old-growth forests are special for their beauty and the diversity of life forms they support, including the thousands of so-called lesser species, of which we know so little, from ground-dwelling fungi to canopy-loving lichen and insects. At least 380 vertebrate wildlife species occur in the coastal rainforest; 262 of them are birds, almost two-thirds of which use old-growth stands to one degree or another for nesting, feeding, or roosting. Threatened species such as the northern spotted owl are especially vulnerable because clearcutting continually shrinks their old-growth habitat, and leaves no hope they will ever get it back. Replanted with selected commercial tree species that grow up as even-aged stands, these second-growth forests may be logged again in fifty years, long before they can regain their old-growth magnificence.

Allowed to generate on its own, an old-growth rainforest becomes a fantastic mosaic supporting a wealth of plant species in various stages of growth and decay. Death has no meaning in these surroundings. Even seemingly lifeless standing snags support a host of wildlife — no fewer than nineteen species of mammals and thirty-seven species of birds, either breeding or hibernating, including squirrels, marten, owls, and woodpeckers — while fallen timber rots and nurses the next generation of rainforest seedlings.

The Portland-based environmental group Ecotrust estimates that almost half the 25 million hectares of coastal temperate rainforests that once covered North America — an area equal to the state of Oregon — has already been lost to logging, agriculture, and other urban development. In the United States portion of that rainforest, only the Elwah River in Washington, Taylor Creek in Oregon, and Big Sur River in California are mostly undeveloped. The policy group World Resources Institute, based in Washington, D.C., found that Canada, Russia, and Brazil house almost 70 percent of the world's remaining original forests, and that only 3 percent of those are located in a temperate zone, representing "the most endangered frontier forests of all." In Washington and Oregon, the institute reports, the total area of old-growth forest now amounts to slightly over one million hectares — just 13 percent of the original amount — of which only about half is protected in national parks or wilderness areas.

The Sierra Club of British Columbia, meanwhile, estimates that more than half of the province's original rainforest has been logged and that no more than 69 of 353 watersheds larger than 5,000 hectares remain in pristine condition. Using the concept of the "Great Bear Rainforest" as their sales pitch, British Columbia conservationists have launched a multi-pronged campaign — using logging road blockades, international boycotts, and political letter writing — to save these final vestiges of old-growth rainforests on the province's remote and sparsely populated central and north coast. A coalition of groups has called for an end to clearcutting and roadbuilding in these last unlogged valleys. A member of the campaign, Greenpeace, argues that half the world's temperate rainforests have been destroyed — a crisis far more urgent than the disappearance of the tropical rainforests — and shifts a greater ecological responsibility onto British Columbia, home to a quarter of what remains.

As both the forest industry and the conservation movement continue to debate how much old growth is enough, it is indisputable that much has already vanished and whatever remains is increasingly vulnerable to clearcut logging. But I am not so jaded by politics or journalism as to believe that the rainforests have reached a point of no return. Not for a minute. To watch a rainforest storm is still one of the world's most life-affirming experiences — at times frightening, always mesmerizing, and, in the end, hope-inspiring.

While researching this book I was rejuvenated by many a rainstorm, but none so awe-inspiring as the storm that struck late one September afternoon at my Prairie Creek campsite in the redwood forests of northern California. As the dark clouds boiled above the upper canopy, I stoked the campfire and huddled beneath a small blue tarp I had suspended with bungee cords from a big-leaf maple. The storm began tentatively enough, neat droplets spilling off the cloud rim, free-falling in slow motion, and landing with grenade force on the hapless creatures inhabiting the miniature world of the forest floor. From my perspective, the temperate rainforest seemed all legs, my pickup truck nothing more than a metallic blue toenail among the gigantic feet of old-growth redwoods and Sitka spruce. As vulnerable as I felt, to venture out would have been suicidal: anyone exposed to these elements for long would almost certainly wilt, liquefy, and eventually leach into the soil to feed the next flush of forest.

As the storm gained momentum, the upper canopy began to sag, and the rain bounced off the exposed roadway with the energy of water on a hot skillet. Strong winds hurried the rain along in undulating waves, vertical sheets of water sidestepped their way through the campsite. Thunder rattled off the rolling mountains with the resounding snap of billiard balls on a hardwood cue. Lightning bolts hurtled across the sky, illuminating the nighttime landscape with the intensity of a neon forest fire. And to make the maelstrom complete, a red alder tree groaned under the weight of the storm, snapped in half, and disintegrated with a thunderous roar just across the creek.

The storm was a tumultuous, humbling spectacle. It was also a moment of spiritual and biological reawakening, a time when the forest seemed born again with the intensity of a revival meeting. I felt the land shudder to life, saw the restless limbs stretch skyward, watched the sword ferns unfurl their emerald scrolls, heard the mushrooms pop out of the ground with the intensity of champagne corks. Bring it on. Let the celebration begin.

# CHAPTER 1

# Seabirds
# on the Edge
*The Sunshine Coast's*
*Marbled Murrelets*

IT IS 4:13 A.M. I should be in my tent. Asleep. Not stumbling through a logging clearcut in darkness with biologist Sandra Webster somewhere in the Bunster Hills above British Columbia's Sunshine Coast. Webster has been here before in search of the marbled murrelet seabird, an elusive and threatened old-growth species. She claims she knows where she is going, even without a flashlight. And she says she's never had a surprise encounter with a bear. But hiking a clearcut is not easy in daylight — slippery logs, sharp tangled brush, discarded cans of engine oil — much less a full hour before sunrise. Our pathway is a minefield of black holes and heavy, protruding objects lit only by the dim glow of dawn.

When we arrive ten minutes later at the upper corner of the clearcut, our warm bodies carving a vapor trail through the cool, still air, we establish ourselves on a prostrate log pressed tight against a remnant forest of yellow cedar, western hemlock, and amabilis fir. It is time to suit up. Even at this early hour, small black clouds of mosquitoes are engulfing our faces, quick to exploit the slightest opening: an exposed ear, the back of a hand, a receding hairline. Nylon-mesh headgear is the only defence, and even then we must wave the bugs off now and again, as if our hands were windshield wipers, just to maintain our field of vision.

Far below us in the distance spread the lights of the Strait of Georgia — tugboats at work, residential communities asleep — part of a protected, inland sea flowing northward from Vancouver between the eastern shore of Vancouver Island and the British Columbia mainland. Just to the north, behind the burly shoulder of the Bunster Range, the strait meets the warm, shallow waters of Desolation Sound, feeding grounds for about 3,000 marbled murrelets. The adult birds fish the sound for sardine-sized sand lances to feed their young — left alone and exposed on mossy limbs somewhere high in the rainforest — and return to the nests every dawn and dusk, when they are least vulnerable to falcons and other predators. It is during these brief deliveries of food that the breeding murrelets are most easily counted by the researchers. And it is the reason Webster has brought me here.

The first thing I discover is that time passes slowly in a clearcut — by definition, a dead zone — especially in the dim morning hours. A varied thrush sounds the first pure notes of a new day, followed by a Wilson's warbler. Then a dark-eyed junco, a nuthatch. Webster knows them all by heart — a simple game of word association, twisting each twitter into an English equivalent. Craning her ear in the direction of an olive-sided flycatcher, she says, "Quick, three beers." Then, before you can say "Wild Turkey," my lesson is interrupted by a sudden thrashing in the brush behind us. No dickie bird this time. We spin around on our log, fully expecting to see a black bear in full charge. Instead — thankfully — it is two black-tailed deer bounding through the underbrush. They were there all the time, frozen in the logging slash, just hoping we were passing through.

Even at this cloaked hour, the irony of our expedition is obvious. Logging of the murrelet's nesting habitat is the reason for the seabird's official status in British Columbia as a threatened species — one short step from endangered, two from complete annihilation in the province. Yet we traveled gravel logging roads for an hour to get here, and we are exploiting the sweeping, open view of a clearcut to study the birds. But this is where irony turns to tragedy. Not only does logging destroy important nesting trees, it also deters murrelet activity because of the loud industrial noise during the summer nesting period. As well, logging can sucker the birds into dangerous nesting practices, such as setting up shop too close to a clearcut. Adept at swimming underwater, murrelets fly through the air like overstuffed chickens, and they land about as gracefully in trees. To these stubby, web-footed birds, clearcuts may seem as welcome as an airport to an aircraft in distress, offering space for landing and takeoff. The problem is that, even in the best of times, 70 percent of murrelet chicks can be killed each year by squirrels, Steller's jays, owls, marten, hawks, eagles, and ravens. Nests built on the edge of a clearcut become all the more vulnerable to predation.

Webster grows restless. Eyes fixed on the open sky, she scans for the smallest sign of life. "Where are they?" she asks. "They should have been here by now." Maybe that's all it took, a little nudge. Seconds later we spot the silhouettes of five adult murrelets. Incoming. Circling. Emitting a high-pitched squeak like a child's plastic squeeze toy. Then they are gone, behind us, lost somewhere in the forests.

Circling behavior is good news, evidence that the birds are still occupying their nests. Evidence that the chicks are still alive. Minutes later, two more adult birds quickly wing their way back toward Desolation Sound. It is just 5:34 a.m. Already the show is over for this morning. It's a disappointing performance. Sightings of adult murrelets reached a height of seventy-five a day one year ago, but total only a third of that this summer. The reason for the poor showing isn't very far away.

The conflict between clearcut logging and wildlife species at risk could not be more pronounced than it is here in the Bunster Range, half a day's drive northwest of Vancouver and the site of an active old-growth logging operation in the midst of the densest nesting habitat for marbled murrelets in North America. The Bunster Range has been selected as the focus for the province's largest bird study, costing a total of $1.7 million over five years. It is an attempt to obtain the most basic information about murrelet breeding, longevity, population, and migration patterns. On the surface, at least, this study by Simon Fraser University's biology department amounts to a truce in the war in the woods, a rare example of cooperation involving funding from the provincial and federal governments and the forest industry. In reality it's pretty much business as usual: continued logging of the continent's greatest murrelet nesting grounds, as though the study did not even exist.

To show me just how desperate the situation has become, Webster drives a short distance uphill to a fresh logging operation by T & T Trucking, a family-owned logging company based in the Sunshine Coast community of Sechelt. A grapple yarder coughing up thick black clouds of diesel smoke is busy hauling felled timber from a clearcut to a landing area for transport by truck off the mountain. Webster cannot get used to the scene. When her research crew set up base camp in the Bunster Range in mid-May for its three-month field season, this was pristine old-growth forest, prime murrelet nesting habitat. Today, less than two months later, about all that remains is a pathetic stand of trees, one old-growth yellow cedar flanked by two small western hemlocks and one amabilis fir, that huddle naked by the exposed roadside. "When we arrived, this was a beautiful forest," Webster laments. "We didn't know it was going to be logged."

The little nesting reserve — voluntarily donated by T & T Trucking — is the brutal reality behind British Columbia's claim to "world-class" logging standards. The yellow cedar is officially nest tree #17. One year earlier it was an active nest site — one of sixty-three known in the region — with two "nest cups" visible on its mossy limbs. Today the tree might as well be a headstone. Any murrelet crazy enough to nest here amid the ongoing racket of chain saws, logging trucks, and grapple yarders would have its egg or chick snapped up in no time by predators. Webster cannot emphasize strongly enough the importance of a good tree. Murrelets are known to decorate the best trees like Christmas ornaments; as many as five murrelet pairs may nest in a single yellow cedar. But #17 has seen its last days. It is useless for another hundred years, until a buffer of second-growth forest grows up around it and offers a cloak of protection. But the wind will blow the big cedar down long before that.

It gets worse. Another prime old-growth nest tree, #19, is gone altogether, logged out, eliminated without a trace. Researchers think the stump of the tree is buried under a new logging road. "We're concerned," Webster says. "The marbled murrelet is bloody difficult enough to study. Little is known about it. Now we risk losing the nest trees and the research along with them. That's the conflict. They're actually logging in the breeding season."

How does T & T Trucking get away with cutting nest trees, an action that would result in charges in, say, California, where logging is banned during the murrelet's breeding season? How, despite the direct participation of the forests ministry and the forest industry in the high-profile murrelet study — the largest, longest, and most intensive in the province — and despite the on-site presence of wildlife researchers, did the nest trees get logged?

According to Steve Gordon, a forest-ecosystem specialist with the British Columbia environment ministry on the Sunshine Coast, forests ministry officials knew full well that T & T Trucking would be cutting into prime marbled murrelet nesting habitat, if not the precise site of individual nest trees. That information, ironically, was held back by environment ministry officials to protect the birds from potential vandals. Should we be surprised? After all, it was Jack Munro, the former IWA-Canada union president, who succinctly voiced his position on endangered species: "I tell my guys if they see a spotted owl to shoot it."

Preferring to look forward rather than rehash the past, Brian Hawrys, operations manager for the Sunshine Coast Forest District in Powell River, insists that lessons have been learned by both sides. Future logging in the Bunster Range will be scaled back, timber crews will leave a 100-metre buffer zone around active nests (but only during the breeding season), and loggers and researchers will work together to coordinate their efforts. "Recognizing there is industrial activity happening there, we want to coordinate to minimize the impact to the birds and researchers," says Hawrys.

But Irene Manley, SFU's top murrelet researcher, counters that none of the forests ministry's promises amount to a long-term plan addressing the habitat needs of the murrelet. "We're still dealing with the issue nest by nest," she says. "It's not murrelet conservation. It's not what the species needs. There's no larger-scale plan happening." The whole fiasco playing out in the Bunster Range raises a key question: if logging of marbled murrelet habitat can occur here, what hope is there for wildlife protection elsewhere in British Columbia, where there are no ongoing studies and no on-site surveillance? "That's one of our concerns," Gordon confirms. "We feel there are lots of key areas that are remote, with not a lot of access or attention."

All of which leads to the larger issue of British Columbia's continued opposition to an endangered-species act, the sort of legislation needed to protect North America's most biologically diverse province or state, which hosts 1,088 vertebrate species, including 458 fresh- and salt-water fish, 448 birds, 143 mammals, 20 amphibians, and 19 reptiles. Due to pressure from the forest industry and the forests ministry, the province delayed for years before releasing watered-down guidelines for an "Identified Wildlife Management Strategy" to deal with rare or endangered species that require an extra level of protection from commercial timber harvesting. Not only do the 1999 guidelines put a cap on protection, allowing no more than one percent of B.C.'s timber supply to be set aside for species at risk from logging, but, for now at least, they officially list only 36 species or subspecies and 4 plant communities, far short of the full list of species at risk, including 152 terrestrial vertebrates, 39 fish, 141 invertebrates, and hundreds of plants and plant communities. Manley suspects that the murrelet would get no more than two 200-hectare patches in the Bunster Range under the new guidelines, a low ecological rating when compared with that for showy species such as grizzly bears.

Fearing the sort of forest-job losses blamed on endangered-species legislation in the U.S. Pacific Northwest — where, it is important to note, the economy is much stronger and unemployment much lower than in British Columbia — Munro's successor as IWA president, the late Gerry Stoney, wrote a letter to the premier's office just five months before the 1996 provincial election. Stoney made it clear that union support for the New Democrats would evaporate if the province brought in similar legislation. Excerpts from that letter, along with a response from Moe Sihota, then the minister of environment, were published in an article in the *Vancouver Sun* in spring 1997. Sihota insisted that the province had no such intentions and that it would leave the matter in federal hands. In a slip that would have embarrassed Freud himself, the minister flatly stated the province would not enact "dangerous species legislation."

Largely unskilled at jobs outside the forest, their ranks vastly diminished by technological change and economics, loggers are understandably unwilling to take another hit to their livelihoods. And their union is not seeking creative new solutions to the jobs-versus-environment debate, having given a cool reception to MacMillan Bloedel Ltd.'s promise to phase out coastal clearcut logging, as we know it, over five years.

Two government initiatives have taken steps toward a more progressive land-use policy: first, a strategy of conserving 12 percent of the provincial land base as parks and protected areas; and second, the Forest Practices Code, legislation that has been repeatedly weakened since its introduction in 1995, but which still strives to reduce logging's footprint on the landscape through measures such as narrower logging roads and smaller landing areas. Both these measures fall far short of ensuring the protection necessary to save the habitat of threatened species.

In a damning wildlife branch internal memo, obtained by the Sierra Legal Defence Fund in September 1998, Greg Jones, the environment ministry's chief of wildlife, said that the ministry's policy on endangered species is full of holes and cannot be defended against the criticism of conservation groups. The ministry does not protect plants and wildlife outside Crown lands, including those damaged by agriculture and cattle grazing, and the Fish Protection Act does nothing for invertebrates and amphibians, including rare frogs, that live in waters not frequented by fish. Finally, endangered-species legislation is needed to ensure that the recommendations of wildlife managers are respected, rather than routinely ignored, by other ministries, especially the forests ministry. "Presently, ministry recommendations are often overruled, resulting in impacts on species at risk," Jones lamented.

For the province to say it is leaving the issue of legislation to the Canadian government is to say it is doing nothing. Despite continuing promises, Ottawa has still not enacted legislation that fully protects the habitat of endangered species — not just federal lands (essentially a handful of national parks, representing 1 percent of British Columbia's land mass) but also provincial Crown land, which constitutes 93 percent of the province's land base, an area greater than the states of Washington, Oregon, and California combined. That leaves conservationists to seek help from the federal Migratory Bird Convention Act, which makes it an offence to "disturb, destroy or take a nest" of a migratory bird. The act cannot stop loggers from showing up and cutting trees used during the previous nesting season, or from making so much noise as to discourage birds from reappearing in the current season. And although the act might save something as large and obvious as a nesting bald eagle, it does nothing for a species as secretive as the marbled murrelet, whose nest is a simple depression on a mossy limb, high in the canopy and invisible to loggers working below.

So secretive is it that Manley and a colleague did not discover British Columbia's first recorded marbled murrelet nest — just a fecal ring on a patch of moss, the chick having already fledged — until 1990. It involved a combination of observation and rope-climbing in a patch of old-growth Sitka spruce at the end of a logging road in the Walbran Valley on Vancouver Island. The discovery showed just how little scientific work had been done in the upper canopy of the rainforest and how little was known about the murrelet. Working today on the Bunster Range project, Manley says murrelets are threatened throughout their range by the degradation of both their marine and nesting areas. As such, their breeding success — or lack of it — is a barometer of environmental change along the interface between ocean and temperate old-growth forest. "The forest on its own won't save them, and neither will the marine habitat," Manley says. "It's the right combination of the two."

Curious to hear loggers' thoughts on the marbled murrelet, I head back downhill at dinner hour to T & T Trucking's camp, a comfortable motor home squeezed alongside the logging road. Several men assembled inside, drinking beer and watching pork chops grill on the outdoor barbecue, offer me a seat and some suds. Although the loggers' conditions are far from luxurious, I have advanced four stars over the researchers' squatter camp a few metres down the muddy hillside. Not only do the researchers sleep in small nylon tents beneath tarps, they also subsist on less-than-ideal rations. When I left them, they were taking whiffs of a four-day-old can of refried beans and offering guesses on its edibility. The juxtaposition is a simple, but indicative, measure of the imbalance of power and money that exists between forestry and environment.

T & T Trucking has the right to extract 19,000 cubic metres of timber at its summer logging operation in the Bunster Range, the result of a sale through the province's small-business program. Most of the timber is western hemlock, with some amabilis fir and yellow cedar, to be used for lumber, pulp, and plywood. Yellow cedar is the *crème de la crème* of the forest, exported almost exclusively to Japan for a combination of structural and cultural uses. Not only is it durable and stable like western red cedar, which is more abundant on the low-lying coast, but due to its slow growth at higher elevations it is denser and stronger, with a finer grain. The Japanese also view it as an equal substitute for their own premier softwood, hinoki, which is used for housing construction and in temples and shrines. With Japan's own supply of hinoki in limited supply, yellow cedar, which represents only about 5 percent of British Columbia's coastal forests, commands top prices. British Columbia's Council of Forest Industries reports that the best grade of yellow cedar logs fetched $327 per cubic metre or an average $126 per cubic metre in January 1999. That is well above an average $112 per cubic metre for western red cedar, $102 for Douglas fir, $70 for spruce, $67 for balsam, $51 for alder, $43 for pine, $37 for maple, and $29 for cottonwood.

An old-growth giant like nest tree #17 — big, but in only fair shape, with some knots and internal rot — would fetch about $5,000, calculates Richard Moase, a log scaler hired on contract by the forests ministry to monitor the stumpage. "I don't think I'm a redneck," he says from the loggers' trailer. "I don't want to kill anything off, but I want to survive, make a good living. How much is a marbled murrelet worth?"

It is the same argument that has been used for generations to justify the exploitation of natural resources for humankind's economic benefit, and it suggests that as a society, our greater perspective on Earth has not evolved that far after all. It also ignores the underlying truth about the interconnectedness of our environment: the demise of the murrelet (not just an individual nesting bird, but the entire species) may not change history, but preserving its old-growth habitat and all its diversity of plants and animals just might. Even more disturbing, however, Moase's question implies that the intrinsic value of a species is an illusion held by a desperate and sentimental conservation movement.

This particular logging crew, like others I have interviewed in recent years, is quick to pat itself on the back. It believes much has changed in the forest, that loggers are more sensitive to the needs of the environment, that the bad old days of rape and pillage are gone forever. After all, didn't these workers voluntarily save that patch of trees just up the hill?

The fact is, you don't have to scratch very far beneath the surface to see that the face of logging hasn't changed that much after all. In the Sunshine Coast town of Powell River, shops still sell postcards featuring the local pulp mill, as though the place was stuck in some industrial, post–Second World War time loop. As far as the murrelet is concerned, the good intentions of this crew extend to a handful of nest trees but not to a buffer of, say, 250 metres, which would provide a realistic measure of protection. "You might as well take the whole timber sale," declares on-site logging manager Bill Trousdell, son of Bob Trousdell, the company founder. "Where do you draw the line? Shut the whole province down?"

Technological advances, global competition, fluctuations of supply and demand, and cold corporate practices are to blame for far more job losses in the province's forests than is environmental conservation. For instance, the IWA's membership in British Columbia, which peaked at 51,000 in 1979, bottomed out at 27,000 in 1991, before the government's policy of protecting 12 percent of the land as parks took effect. Still, the murrelet makes an easy target.

Loggers, I have also found, are quick to substitute their own anecdotal observations for the meticulous analysis of scientists. If they see a bear foraging in a clearcut, then clearcuts must be good for bears. Never mind what happens fifteen years down the road, when the single-aged stand closes in and converts the forest floor to darkness, incapable of sustaining much of anything. As for the murrelets, they are routinely spotted bobbing on the ocean surface, so the population must be okay.

What's the big deal? "The British Columbia coast has been logged for 100 years," says Moase, playing down the industry's impact on murrelets. "It's been burned down many times over thousands of years. So I'm not so sure." It is an argument that ignores the fact that fires are nature's way of kickstarting the natural regeneration of old-growth forests, whereas clearcutting prevents the regeneration of a natural forest. The sheer scale of industrial logging also extinguishes the forest fire argument — 190,000 hectares clearcut in the province in 1996, compared with 14,952 hectares burned.

The loggers are equally unconvinced that clearcuts tilt the odds against a murrelet chick, saying it's ludicrous to suggest a raven cannot find a murrelet even deep in the forest. And they suggest that the occasional use of helicopters by researchers to reach inaccessible areas of the Sunshine Coast, along with the practice of netting birds for tagging, may cause far more disruption than an ill-timed chainsaw. "It's difficult," Moase says. "I'm not sure who's more offensive to the birds."

Late the next afternoon I arrive by truck at a small dock in Okeover Inlet, one of the fluid fingers extending from the hand of Desolation Sound. Known far and wide for its warm, sheltered waters, the sound is also something of a cultural melting pot. Part of it is a provincial marine park, a magnet for touring yachters and pleasure boaters from throughout the Pacific Northwest; the other part is the domain of eighteen commercial oyster growers — "a bunch of over-the-hill hippies," as they call themselves — holding water lots leased from the province and living in all manner of ships, shacks, cabins, and even the odd remnant geodesic dome. It is a place to expect the unexpected, a vortex of colliding worlds from which the fate of the marbled murrelet may eventually emerge.

Cecilia Lougheed is waiting for me, dressed in a bright-orange marine survival suit, binoculars around her neck, and at the helm of a small motorized inflatable craft. She is studying for her master's degree in wildlife ecology and she is responsible for observing the murrelets on their feeding grounds and identifying specific birds based on artificial markings — colored nasal disks, color patches, and radio transmitters.

A native of Ecuador, she grew up on Santa Cruz Island in the Galapagos Islands, moved to Quito — the country's mainland capital — at age fifteen for her education, and later returned to the Galapagos to study masked boobies on Española Island in 1994. That's where she fell in love with her future husband, Canadian Lynn Lougheed, who was researching his master's thesis on blue-footed boobies on the same island. A year later Cecilia and Lynn returned to British Columbia to study the marbled murrelet. Climate, vegetation, and culture aside, the elusive murrelet poses a challenge she had not encountered in the Galapagos. "I used to get out of my tent and walk five minutes to be in a colony of 10,000 pairs," she says. "It was completely different, everything right there."

As we motor out of Okeover Inlet toward Lancelot Inlet, following the eastern shoreline, several murrelets pop up. Occasionally the surface of the ocean will boil with schools of sand lances trying to escape the birds hunting them from below. Close to dusk, the murrelets swim through the schools, staying underwater for thirty to sixty seconds at a time, in search of the biggest and fattest fish to feed their chicks waiting in the mountain forests. When it is finally time to leave, the murrelets flap their wings like clumsy bats, slowly building up speed while bouncing their bellies against the water surface. Eventually they manage to fly through the air with the trajectory of a poorly thrown football. Given the energy they expend in flight — not just in getting off the water, but in navigating all the way up the Bunster Range to their nests — it is obvious why they seek out the biggest fish possible.

Looking through her binoculars, Lougheed spots a bird with yellow paint on its tail feathers, an orange nasal tag on the left side of its beak, yellow on its right, and emitting a recognized radio-telemetry frequency from an antenna glued to its wing. It is a bird captured and tagged on June 25, just nine days ago. This sort of work is key to developing a life history of this elusive bird and estimating its population changes. What researchers are learning is that the adults patrol the inner inlets, closest to the rainforest nesting areas, during the April-to-October breeding season, but once the chicks are fledged and on their own, the birds drift farther out from shore. They are also known to migrate between Canadian and American waters and to return to the same nesting grounds year after year.

Although the murrelets do not undertake extensive migrations, they are a species whose survival depends on international cooperation. One bird banded in 1995 at Desolation Sound was captured off Washington's Orcas Island in 1996 and recaptured at Desolation Sound in 1997. "It's very difficult and very frustrating working with the marbled murrelet," Lougheed confides as we pull into the research base camp near the mouth of Theodosia Inlet. "But it's also very rewarding."

Little more than a knuckle extending eastward from the digit of Lancelot Inlet, Theodosia is a narrow, shallow body of water with a blind, bottleneck entrance. To the murrelets, Theodosia Inlet forms an obvious runway from the kitchen to the bedroom, a convenient funnel between marine feeding habitat and old-growth nesting habitat. To the research team it is an equally logical place to lie in wait, ready to wring the most basic biological information out of these soggy little seabirds.

The research camp, located on land rented for $2,500 a year from one of the oyster growers, consists of two rectangular tents lit by batteries that are recharged by generators. One tent is a mess hall and meeting area, the other is for research. Every day, as part of a study to determine the exact period in which females lay their eggs, the team takes the vials of blood extracted from the murrelets and uses a centrifuge to separate the red blood cells from the plasma. The former's DNA is tested to determine sex; the latter is tested for a hormonal signature — triglycerides the consistency of buttermilk — that shows the female bird is creating an egg.

As dusk approaches, Lynn Lougheed assembles eight researchers in two inflatables, then motors to the mouth of the inlet. Working in two teams, the biologists attach "mist" nets to floats stretching across the inlet entrance. The nets are laid out in two parallel but staggered lines that allow enough room for passing vessels to navigate through with the aid of red and green navigational beacons. That's the theory, anyway. Occasionally the nets snag a drunken, cursing oyster grower trying to find his way home by boat in darkness and refusing the researchers' efforts to guide him through the maze.

On Susan Islet, a patch of rock on the south side of Theodosia, sits a small, green tent beneath a blue tarp and an arbutus tree. Taking me to the tent for a first-hand look, Lougheed opens the front flap to expose the most covert part of the research operation — a radar system once used by the SeaBus, the marine transit system in Vancouver's Burrard Inlet, and now on loan from the Canadian Wildlife Service. Operated by a small generator, the radar unit ensures that even birds flying over the netting are monitored — their radar-screen image captured by a video camera also mounted inside the tent. Outside, the only evidence of radar is the antenna, twitching like a suspended dragonfly in the waning light.

For researchers, radar is an efficient way of counting murrelets. On average it spots 25 percent more than the human eye and allows them to spot a subtle decline in population before the species gets into serious trouble. Important stuff, considering that murrelet pairs raise just one chick per year. And although the odds are stacked against that one's survival, early estimates show that adults have an 85 percent chance of living to see the next year — the sort of imbalance you'd expect from a species with a low birth rate. But Lougheed warns, "It takes a long time for them to come back if the population gets in trouble. You can't grow old-growth trees in the life span of a bird."

Once the mist nets are strung out across the inlet, the researchers retreat to a nearby dock; set up a table full of needles, vials, and other banding supplies; and wait for the first victim to become entangled in the web. It doesn't take long. At 9:08 p.m. an adult murrelet is lodged nose-first in the netting, so surprised by its capture that the sand lance is still in its black, tweezer-like beak. Removed from its snare, the bird is placed in a small blue bag with a white drawstring and is taken to the table for processing. This particular bird is the 208th capture this year; allowing for repeat captures, it's the 175th murrelet.

The table is a good place to observe the bird, which weighs in somewhere between a robin and a pigeon. The webbed feet on this particular murrelet show only minimal wear, evidence that it is probably a young adult. Its beady eyes are ink black, its back feathers brown with white speckles, becoming mottled on the chest — the marble in the murrelet — fading to white on the belly. Near the bottom is a brood patch the size of a silver dollar, where the mother's warm, exposed skin is pressed against the egg. Once the chick is hatched and the brooding process is finished, the down grows back.

Blood is extracted from the brachial vein under one of the wings. A feather is plucked, as part of another DNA experiment. Yellow and purple tags, designed to fall off during molt in six weeks, are fitted on the murrelet's wings with waterproof cement. A transmitter with a miniature antenna — valued at $200 and powerful enough to be monitored from two kilometres away — is glued to the bird's back. Yellow dye is dabbed on the bird's butt. Colored nasal disks are sewn to each side of its beak with fishing line. The body, feathers, and bill are measured, and a stainless steel band with an identification number and address is clamped around one of its feet.

The exhaustive process takes close to one hour. "It's equivalent to an alien abduction," concedes researcher Brad Vanderkist. Since 1991, when the Canadian Wildlife Service started banding marbled murrelets in Desolation Sound, there have been 1,270 captures in mist nets or dip nets at night with lights, including 140 repeat captures. During that time, only five birds have keeled over dead from the stress — a sad number, considering the goal is to spare the birds from clearcut logging, but considered unavoidable if researchers are to obtain the basic information they need for the species management.

When the research team is finally finished, Lougheed takes the bird to the end of the dock and releases it skyward with exaggerated flair. Then, almost on cue, a loud explosion unexpectedly reverberates across the still waters of Desolation Sound, followed by a multi-colored burst in the sky above Mink Island, about five kilometres to the northwest. It is the Fourth of July, and Americans staying on the island are celebrating Independence Day. The researchers, skilled at observation, cannot help but remark that July 1, Canada Day, went off without a peep.

The fireworks are unexpected, but maybe they're appropriate for the beleaguered marbled murrelet, a migratory species whose future depends as much on events in the U.S. as in Canada. As for bird #208, now disappearing into the darkness, the fact that it can still fly under the weight of such scientific study is perhaps cause for celebration. That it might provide scientists with another clue in the larger puzzle of its mysterious life is indeed grounds for optimism.

CHAPTER 2

# Written
# in the Wood
*The Western Red
Cedars of Cascadia*

THREE CENTURIES AFTER the last great earthquake rumbled
through the Pacific Northwest, drowning aboriginal villages and their
inhabitants, kicking the legs out from under the temperate rainforest,
and hurling a tsunami across the ocean at the speed of a passenger jet,
a few dozen witnesses still provide mute testimony to that cataclysmic
event on the muddy banks of the lower Copalis River. Finding them
is as easy as making your way to the small razor-clamming resort of
Copalis Beach in western Washington state and launching a canoe
across the street from Larry's Cafe and the miniature golf course.
Then paddle upstream, around the Highway 109 bridge pilings and
past the rusting car parts badgered into the shoreline, until, fifteen
minutes later, you reach the undulating field of tufted hairgrass on
your left side. There you are.

29

At first the field looms like some sort of abandoned aboriginal site, not unlike the Haida peoples' Ninstints on the Queen Charlotte Islands of British Columbia, a remnant collection of totem poles in various sizes and shapes, but all old and gray and broken. Only as you approach closer, however, do you realize these are not totems at all, but the forlorn, decaying bodies of a once magnificent stand of western red cedars. It is tempting to call the place an arboreal cemetery, but it would be inaccurate. The tree may die, but its energy continues. It simply changes form, shifts shape, and is born again into a new and equally important identity in the cycle of life. Consider these Goliaths standing before me, in death giving life to new generations — a mat of salal, a sprig of Sitka, a flush of sweet huckleberries, already sprouting from the productive mulch of the cedars' sweet rotting skin. And when these giants finally do collapse with a final, thunderous roar, falling face down in the muddy salt marsh, they will live on as a breeding ground for insects, a reservoir for moisture during summer's drought, a foothold for fungi to convert their woody torso into soil to perpetuate the next generation of rainforest.

That these cedars continue to stand three centuries after their official death is a testament to the unique and potent chemicals with which they are saturated, providing a natural resistance to insects and disease. In their purest form these chemicals are capable of dissolving stainless steel and are an equal match for the highly toxic pentachlorophenols, or PCPs, once used as wood preservatives in the lumber industry. The cedar's natural chemicals have proven equally toxic to humans: workers in cedar mills and horticultural operations are at risk of contracting asthma from breathing cedar dust or developing skin rashes from handling the wood — as my own family can confirm. My father, Art, suffered severe rashes on his arms while working at a New Westminster cedar mill in the 1960s, a key factor in his return to work as a bridge-and-ballast foreman with BC Rail. Twenty years later my sister Kathy was forced to quit her job at a Mission nursery for the same reasons. It took a full month for the incessant itching to stop and the facial swelling to subside. "I reached the point my eyes were tiny slits in my puffy face," she recalls today with a lingering wince. "I was embarrassed to go to the doctor's office. But he said if I'd gone a few days later, it might have been too late."

These same chemicals work to preserve red cedar after death, like embalming fluid, delaying its decay by a matter of decades. The big ancient cedars of the Fraser Valley had been logged long before my father and mother, Frances, moved onto their small homestead in south Aldergrove, after the Second World War. But the stumps of those trees — even the oldest ones, gnawed away by internal rot and ravaged by one weekend bonfire after another — refused to concede defeat. On one of the burliest stumps we installed a small hinged door, through which the children could enter its inner sanctum. But even our fertile imaginations could not have envisioned the day a motorist headed for the Canada–United States border would make the mistake of stashing several bottles of beer inside our stump, returning home to find his donation graciously accepted, his empties ready for pickup, and, as a trespasser on our land, with no avenue of recourse.

The western red cedar's reputation for longevity makes it highly desirable to scientists researching everything from the rise of coastal aboriginal culture to the tracking of weather trends, from the evolution of the temperate rainforest to the impact of global warming. For Brian Atwater, the ancient forest of the Copalis River also holds the final clue to unravelling the mystery of the region's last great earthquake. While other trees have been rendered to dust, the cedars live on, providing a natural storehouse of information for those who know how to read them. As a geologist with the United States Geological Survey and an affiliate professor at the University of Washington in Seattle, Atwater is helping to create a new understanding of the fragile rainforest, offering fresh insight into a catastrophic natural event that occurred almost 300 years ago and ringing the wake-up alarm for us all to prepare for the next big earthquake to hit the Pacific Northwest. "It's been a detective game," he agrees, pulling his canoe into the spongy riverbank. "This erases any real doubt as to these events happening. It's not a figment of a geologist's imagination."

The Copalis is more of a brackish, tidal slough than a true river. It is a refuge from humanity, its peacefulness shattered only by the machine-gun rat-a-tat-tat of a belted kingfisher in flight. There is little to draw people here — except, perhaps, the unexpected. In March 1998 a hunter scouting for black-bear tracks claimed to have discovered two strange sets of human-like prints, prompting a plaster-casting expedition of enthusiasts dedicated to the Sasquatch, the mythical ape man of the Pacific Northwest.

In a sense, the Copalis River does co-exist with an invisible giant, flowing as it does through the Cascadia subduction zone, a geologic hot spot responsible not just for earthquakes but for igneous rock formations, natural hotsprings, and a chain of snow-draped volcanoes that include Mount Rainier in Washington state and, north of the border, Mount Garibaldi near Whistler ski resort. Think of the Cascadia zone as a ragged line on the ocean floor — the point at which the Juan de Fuca plate shoehorns its way beneath the larger North American plate — extending for more than 600 miles from the west coast of Vancouver Island south down to northern California. The Cascadia zone is more active than central California's infamous San Andreas fault but displays its might less frequently, preferring to percolate quietly beneath the surface, sometimes for centuries, before erupting with a frightening, awe-inspiring display. The most recent outburst occurred in 1980, in southern Washington. The dramatic eruption of Mount St. Helens killed 57 persons, wiped out 220 homes and 27 bridges, flattened about 375 square miles of wilderness, and coughed gritty ash twelve miles into the air.

Although geologists have developed early-warning detection systems for volcanic eruptions — eighty-three-year-old Harry Truman assumed folk-hero status for ignoring warnings to leave his home beneath Mount St. Helens, only to be buried alive in the mud and ash — earthquake forecasting remains a dark science. But the western red cedars of the Copalis River are providing the first clues by allowing scientists to accurately date the timing of past eruptions.

After a decade of studies on both sides of the Pacific Ocean, an international research team including members from the United States, Japan, and Canada has finally calculated the timing of the last great earthquake with eerie accuracy — 9 p.m., January 26, 1700. The earthquake was huge, a "megathrust" quake, which, scientists suggest, would have registered 9 on today's Richter scale. That is a hundred times more destructive than the San Francisco earthquake of 1989, an event that brought one of America's richest cities to its knees, crippling sewer, water, and transportation services, and filling churches with God-fearing converts. Unlike the Bay Area disaster, however, the quake of 1700 did not have an epicenter as we know it, but ripped open the subduction zone along the entire coast. The rumbling and creaking would have lasted for more than a minute, an eternity to the tens of thousands of aboriginal people who flourished on the Pacific Northwest coast then.

When the thunder finally stopped, it was followed by a tsunami — a wall of water and sand that would have inundated the North American coastline while simultaneously fanning out across the Pacific Ocean. Despite traveling at jet speed, the violent pulse of water would have generated little more than a ripple as it swept through the immensity of the open ocean, rising up as a formidable juggernaut only as it approached the shoreline.

During that brief moment on the Copalis River, the land collapsed with the release of pressure pent-up for centuries. The shoreline sank and exposed the roots of the rainforest — and the cedars — to a fatal dose of salt water. Over the ensuing 300 years the tidal action hid all traces of the event with a thick, oozing blanket of silt. To prove the point, Atwater bites into the riverbank with a small shovel and exposes three neat layers as distinct as Neapolitan ice cream: a bottom layer of brown organic earth on which the rainforest once grew, a middle layer of gray sand deposited by the tsunami, and a finishing layer of olive-colored mud deposited by the river.

British Columbia is located at the northern end of the subduction zone, where the land dropped less than it did on the Copalis River. Still, Canadian researchers have unearthed similar evidence of layering at Tofino and Ucluelet on the west coast of Vancouver Island, as well as finding sand volcanoes — thin vertical veins of sand that indicate violent shaking of the earth — in drainage ditches in the Fraser River delta near Vancouver.

Evidence supporting the eruption of 1700 is also derived from the aboriginal peoples of the Pacific Northwest. Aboriginal legend on Vancouver Island tells of a terrifying shaking of the earth one winter night long ago and of a village at Pachena Bay, near the present town of Bamfield, that was wiped out by the tsunami that followed. "They describe how, at night, the ground shook," confirms John Clague, a geologist with the Geological Survey of Canada. "Shortly after, a huge flood destroyed the village. Everyone was killed."

None of this evidence is as compelling as the teetering fossil forest on the Copalis River. Battered for three centuries by wind and rain cartwheeling off the Pacific Ocean, the stumps have been stripped of their skin and telltale outer growth rings, forcing scientists to look underground at root systems still neatly preserved in an ancient burial chamber of mud. Atwater dons his yellow waterproof pants, cinches down his orange hardhat with the ear protectors and face guard, and lowers himself into a coffin-sized hole dug beneath the trunk of a cedar stump. Then he fires up a small chainsaw and confidently carves off a fireplace-sized chunk of root. Brushing away the mud with his glove, he points to a stringy section of salmon-colored bark — evidence that the cedar's latest growth rings are still intact. "There you have it," he beams. "You can see how well it is preserved." Through radiocarbon dating, scientists have been able to estimate with 95 percent confidence that the cedars died between 1695 and 1710. And by counting the unmistakable annual growth rings on the root system, they have concluded the cedars died shortly after the fall of 1699.

For the final piece of the puzzle, scientists reached across the Pacific Ocean to Japan, a nation with a long history of earthquake activity and a wealth of written records. Research by the Geological Survey of Japan and the Earthquake Research Institute of the University of Tokyo found reference to a tsunami that struck at least five villages at about midnight on January 27, 1700. Most of the damage seems to be minor — inundation of coastal rice paddies and damage to some homes and storehouses. The greatest impact occurred in Miyako, a seaside town about 300 miles north of Tokyo, where twenty homes were damaged.

When Japanese scientists conducted an on-site investigation of the five villages, they concluded that the even distribution pattern in the soils left by the waves could only be consistent with an offshore tsunami. Further evidence pointing to the tsunami's North America origin was the tendency of typhoons to inundate coastal Japanese towns seasonally, from August to October. On the day the communities were hit by the wall of water, the weather was described in the records as clear and sunny — and not a mention of local seismic activity.

Convinced that the tsunami originated in the Cascadia subduction zone, the scientists made a number of calculations that accounted for the level of damage caused in Japan and for the ten hours
of traveling time across the Pacific. Their conclusion? A magnitude-9
earthquake occurred on the west coast of North America at approximately 9 p.m. on January 26, 1700 — a perfect match for the jigsaw
posed by the preserved roots on the Copalis River.

No sooner had scientists solved one puzzle, however, than they
were faced with an even more daunting one: trying to predict when
the next megathrust quake would occur. With guesses ranging from
tomorrow to 500 years, there is no sense of urgency on the West
Coast to upgrade building-code standards or even commit to personal preparedness. "Earthquakes don't go off like clockwork," Clague
agrees. "For some reason, they don't have that regularity, and that's
what makes it difficult. But there is no such thing as being completely prepared. We always have to strive to be better prepared for one
when it does occur — and it certainly will."

That the western red cedar should play such a pivotal research
role in the geologic history of the Pacific Northwest seems fitting.
Throughout the length of North America's Pacific coast, from southeast Alaska to northern California, the red cedar is the elder of the
temperate rainforest. It is capable of swelling to about 60 feet in circumference, reaching almost 200 feet in height, and living more than
a thousand years. Tolerant of shady, wet conditions that would deter
most other trees, the red cedar thrives in low-lying coastal regions
where mild temperatures and abundant rainfall allow for year-round
photosynthesis and provide a protective barrier against the ravages of
wildfire.

Anyone who has walked the rainforests of the Pacific Northwest
cannot help but recognize the western red cedar, the official tree of
British Columbia. The trunk is strong, fluted, and buttressed to

counteract the effects of high winds. The root system is tangled and opportunistic, linking arms with its subterranean neighbors in an act of solidarity. Its grayish-brown bark is fibrous and stringy, its needles flat and glossy green. And while its spindly top inevitably dies from nutrient deficiency, it is quick to sprout a replacement and over time to create a tuning-fork or candelabra effect. Despite these common traits, however, the cedar is more individualistic than any other rain-forest tree, assuming a bulbous and misshapen profile as it puts on girth and age. Perhaps that's why it is the most frequently hugged tree in the rainforest, possessing human-like qualities that remind us of our own imperfections.

Historically the western red cedar represented the cultural life-blood of coastal aboriginal tribes. Soft, lightweight, and easy to work with, red cedar ranked with the salmon as the coast's most important natural resource. The bark was used for kindling, dye, baskets, mats, and clothing; the wood for masks, bowls, and other carvings, and as planks for buildings. Whole trees were used for posts, logs, and dug-out canoes. Native people knew it as "long life maker" (which closely compares with Europeans' *arbor-vitae*, Latin for "tree of life"), and one Coast Salish legend tells of the Great Spirit creating red cedar in honor of a generous person who bestowed food and clothing on others.

Today the commercial uses of red cedar continue to increase, as shakes and shingles, exterior siding and trim boards, fencing, patio decking, and high-end interior trim. Western red cedar accounts for a fifth of British Columbia's coastal timber harvest — a slightly higher proportion than Douglas fir, but about one-third the volume of west-ern hemlock and balsam fir, which are sold as a single unit on com-mercial markets. The Western Red Cedar Lumber Association, the marketing arm of United States and Canadian producers, just can't get enough of cedar. It is considered a high-end niche market because

of its beauty, durability, and a straight grain that prevents warping —
features equally as important to the aboriginal carver practicing an
ancient tradition as to the do-it-yourself home handyman. But as
much as industry would like to abandon the notion of biodiversity for
a monoculture forest of pure red cedar, nature will have no part of it.
Red cedar grows best in the shade, regenerating when and how it
likes, which is one reason why the species represents only 5 percent of
the 240 million commercial seedlings produced annually in British
Columbia. "Every cedar trees puts off about 200,000 seeds per year in
its cones," explains the association's executive director, Ken McClel-
land, whose North Vancouver backyard is one recipient of the wind-
fall. "It's prolific in that way. At any time, I've got twenty trees that are
eighteen inches tall. I've got to pull the stupid things out like weeds or
they'll just take over."

Any examination of the modern role of red cedar, however, would
not be complete without a sense of where the species originated and
where it is headed. To that end, scientists peeling back the layers of
Earth's convoluted geologic history are finding that the rainforest is
not stable at all, but is an ecosystem in flux, a product of continuing
changes in soil and temperature and precipitation. The concept be-
muses and challenges the likes of Richard Hebda, something of a
unique and complex life form himself, both passionate and animated
about his field of endeavor. Officially he is curator of botany and
earth history at the Royal British Columbia Museum in Victoria and
an adjunct associate professor in biology and earth and ocean sciences
at the University of Victoria. But he is content with the designation
"time traveller," a scientist who has carved a career out of investigat-
ing the temperate rainforest. "What do they call me?" he says. "I'm
just somebody who studies the ecology of past times."

Research has taken him to almost a dozen bogs and lakes
throughout Vancouver Island, from sea level to subalpine, from the

Brooks Peninsula to Port Hardy. Working all day in the pouring rain and sopping mud, Hebda is often found sinking a yard-long cylindrical tube up to fifteen yards deep into the bowels of the earth, probing the ancient sediments for clues to past climates and landscapes. The pollen and spores shed by ancient forests were carried by wind and water and deposited into the bogs, where they represent neatly preserved scientific specimens. Once resurrected for radio carbon dating and microscopic identification, they can create a broad-brush portrait of past worlds.

Hebda's research suggests that open grassland and lodgepole pine were the first to pioneer the land, emerging after the last ice age retreated about 14,000 years ago. The true temperate rainforest, consisting of western hemlock, balsam fir, Douglas fir, Sitka spruce, and, last on the scene, red cedar, became firmly established in only the past 2,000 to 4,000 years, after the climate moderated, rainfall increased, and soils developed. But of all the rainforest species, it is the cedar that has had the greatest cultural influence, signalling a profound turning point for aboriginal people inhabiting the Pacific Northwest. The earliest archaeological information from coastal aboriginal middens reveals mostly shells and other evidence of a marine-based diet. But all that changed about 2,500 years ago. Consistent with the discovery of extensive deposits of red cedar pollen in bogs, scientists found the first evidence of huge wooden aboriginal longhouses and specialized tools such as mauls and wedges. Says Hebda, "It was an environmental revolution that provided an opportunity for cultural development."

Of course, as with the earthquake of 1700, the practical importance of unearthing past climatic forces is to predict events yet to come. True, research into the temperate rainforest since the last ice age clearly shows that dramatic climatic change is a natural process. But there is nothing natural about the speed of change caused by today's cocktail of pollution, industrial activity, and population growth. We know it as global warming — rising temperatures that result from increased emissions of greenhouse gases such as carbon dioxide, the byproduct of burning fossil fuels, including wood, petroleum, coal, and natural gas. Natural? Clearly not. Inevitable? Apparently so. Nations are admitting defeat on a commitment made at the United Nations Earth Summit in 1992 to cap greenhouse gas emissions at 1990 levels by 2000 and instead are turning their focus to limiting the effects of change.

Some scientists fear that change has already begun in the temperate rainforests of North America. Consistent with unusually warm weather trends across the continent (1998 was Canada's warmest year on record, 2.5 degrees Celsius above normal), foresters in southeast Alaska have noticed a marked decline in yellow cedar, a slow-growing, mid- to high-elevation species that is capable of living for 1,500 years. Although scientists initially suspected fungal disease and beetle infestation, they have now turned their attention to subtle changes in soil conditions associated with global warming.

The fate of the yellow cedar could be a foreshadowing. In the absence of effective pollution controls, levels of carbon dioxide are expected to double from pre-industrial times within the next eighty years. Throughout the great inland sea that includes the Strait of Georgia and Puget Sound, temperatures are predicted to rise by 4 to 5 degrees Celsius in winter and 3 to 4 degrees in summer, enough to wreak havoc with weather patterns. Rainfall could increase by 40 percent in winter, flooding out residents in low-lying areas, increasing slope instability on logging clearcuts, even leaving some ski resorts hopelessly green year-round as the altitude at which freezing occurs rises. Summer precipitation could drop by 25 percent, resulting in water shortages for hydroelectric power, residential use, and agricultural irrigation; increasing smog or low-level ozone around urban areas; and damaging salmon spawning runs by reducing flows and raising water temperatures in coastal streams.

Unlike farmers, who can experiment with new crops every year in an attempt to bob and weave with the punch of climatic change, commercial foresters are faced with the daunting task of having to plant seedlings today that might not be harvested for close to a century. Under one optimistic scenario, increased levels of carbon dioxide could actually work as a fertilizer to promote growth, expanding the range of tree species currently limited by cold several hundred miles northward and several hundred yards up mountainsides.

On the other hand, troublesome new pests and huge forest fires could counteract the gains. Plant and animal species already at the edge of their range, teetering on the brink of survival, could be lost. The growth of seedlings planted in spring would be seriously hampered by a 20 percent decrease in rainfall, a situation worsened even further in areas that depend on snowmelt. Foresters are thinking about changing their planting schedules, removing extraneous plants that might compete with seedlings for moisture, increasing the density and genetic makeup of seedlings, lengthening rotations between cuts, reducing harvests, and even moving away from clearcutting to reduce soil surface temperatures.

In the game of ecological sweepstakes, scientists are hedging their bets, still unsure how the temperate rainforest will respond to sharp and drastic climatic change. Ron Neilson is a bioclimatologist with the United States Forest Service, a professor at Oregon State University in Corvallis, and America's leading prognosticator of climate change. Does he envisage California redwoods growing on the Olympic Peninsula? Saguaro cactus sprouting in eastern Washington? For all his expertise, Neilson is very much in the dark about the rainforest's future, still uncertain whether the pendulum will swing toward a drier or wetter climate and wondering how a species whose genetics are specific to one site will adapt to moving hundreds of miles north-ward. Will it grow? Can it reproduce? How will it get there? "If you plant them now, they won't be adapted to today's climate," Neilson adds. "If you wait till then to plant them, the rug is still moving out from under them. We don't see any good way to address it."

Some experts believe that the northern range of the Douglas fir, which now extends to the mid-coast of British Columbia, will expand under climate change, while that of western hemlock, a species vul-nerable to drought, will decline. As for the western red cedar — an ecological socialite, capable of existing alongside hemlock as well as drier forests of Douglas fir — it should do just fine. The greater spec-tre, scientists warn, is the effect of sudden climate change combined with the effects of clearcut logging. Exactly how much abuse can the system take before collapsing under the weight of human folly? "It's the double whammy," Hebda confirms. "You bring about enormous stress on organisms and ecosystems. It's the scope and the extent of change."

On the Copalis River, meanwhile, the small grove of ancient red cedars waited patiently for three centuries for someone to unlock its memories of a brief natural event that altered the rainforest landscape. While the forces unleashed by climate change will display neither the speed nor the obviousness of a magnitude-9 earthquake, their effects are almost certain to be broader, harsher, and more destructive to our environment. If climate change indeed has a parallel to the last great quake to rumble through the Pacific Northwest, it is the unavoidable truth that when it arrives, it will be too late to act.

CHAPTER 3

# Winter of
# the Devil Bear

*Wolverines of the
Columbia Mountains*

TERRIBLE TED WAS a wolverine with an attitude. Captured in a live trap in Woolsey Creek in the Columbia Mountains near Revelstoke, in southeastern British Columbia, he kicked up a frightful fuss before researchers could sedate him with a drug-laced needle and secure a radio-collar transmitter around his thick, furry neck. Relieved to see the cantankerous beast finally sent on his way, the researchers had no way of knowing that just two weeks later they would meet Terrible Ted again in an incident that would only add to the long and legendary catalogue of wolverine stories from the heart of the Canadian wilderness.

At first the biologists conducting a routine radio-telemetry flight to trace the wolverine's movements spotted a small patch of blood on the snowy subalpine mountainside. Only when they approached for a closer look, touching down in a swirl of snow with their chartered helicopter, did the full magnitude of Terrible Ted's strength, endurance, and voracity begin to emerge.

There lay the bloody carcass of a bull mountain caribou, 300 pounds of prey that Terrible Ted had managed to track and kill alone. The caribou had not been in perfect health. A closer inspection showed researchers that the animal had a broken shoulder blade and several damaged vertebrae, but those were old injuries, probably from a cougar or a grizzly bear attack a year earlier. Since then the caribou had survived just fine, thank-you . . . until Terrible Ted came loping across the landscape, precipitating one of the biggest and most dramatic mismatches of the Interior rainforest.

Just imagine. The caribou is bedded down in the deep snow, quietly digesting a meal of lichen, when it spots the wolverine's diminutive 25 pounds of fur and muscle rambling toward it. Ted does not look so terrible from a distance. So the caribou, an animal that is naturally too curious for its own good, stays put, watches, and waits. And that is its fatal mistake. Before the caribou can react, the wolverine quickly skims across the snow on wide, flat paws and lunges at his prey, landing on its back and tenaciously hanging on to its neck. Judging by the blood and depressions in the snow, nature's system of justice proved to be no different than our own — neither swift nor certain — and accomplished over a period of hours, if not days, as the wolverine's powerful jaws clenched against the back of the caribou's neck.

That the battle lasted as long as it did is a testament as much to the caribou as to the wolverine. This I learned from personal experience during a hike six years earlier in the Northwest Territories. On the barren grounds of the Mackenzie Mountains I came across the antlers of a bull caribou that had become ensnared in telephone wire abandoned during a Second World War military project. I could scarcely bend the wire with my bare hands, yet the caribou had managed to tightly wind at least thirty yards of the stuff around its antlers before collapsing in exhaustion, an easy meal for an opportunistic carnivore, perhaps even a wolverine.

When Terrible Ted's battle with his own caribou finally ended, he wasted no time savoring the victory. Following the instinct of his species, he immediately went to work dismembering the carcass, then caching each chunk deep in the snow, a well-stocked refrigerator to which he could return time and again during the lean months of winter. On the day the research biologists arrived, the wolverine had already chewed through the caribou's vertebrae with guillotine efficiency and dragged the severed head across the snow to the base of a tree. "Terrible Ted used to like caribou, and he would always follow their tracks," recalls John Krebs, a BC Hydro biologist in charge of the province's first study of the elusive creature. "Its bite is so powerful — once it latched on, it would be very difficult to get it off."

Of all the creatures to inhabit North America's temperate rainforest, none is more mysterious or misunderstood than the wolverine. Known to scientists as *Gulo gulo luscus* — the gluttonous one — the animal is called devil bear, carcajou, devil beast, and skunk bear. It is the largest terrestrial member of the weasel, or mustelid, family. It resembles a furry badger, measures about three feet from nose to tail, and weighs on average up to 33 pounds for males, 22 pounds for females. Although wolverines spend most of their time scavenging, employing a keen sense of smell to find their food, they are also opportunistic predators capable of killing larger mammals such as caribou. But they usually eat smaller prey, including ground squirrels, birds, marmots, even porcupines, and subsist on insects and berries during the lean times.

Tales of the wolverine's prowess are legendary among wilderness travelers. In 1906 the artist and naturalist Ernest Thompson Seton wrote: "Picture a weasel — and most of us can do that, for we have met that little demon of destruction, that small atom of insensate courage, that symbol of slaughter, sleeplessness, and tireless, incredible activity — picture that scrap of demoniac fury, multiply that mite some fifty times, and you have the likeness of a wolverine." Trappers describe the wolverine as especially crafty once it evades a 330 Conibear killing trap, returning with impunity time and time again to pilfer bait or consume the carcasses of other trapped furbearers. The *Canadian Trappers Manual* confirms the wolverine's "tendency for destroying traps and their fur-bearing content" and for accidentally getting caught in traps set for other furbearers. For those planning to skin the wolverine carcass for a rug or wall mount, the manual has a small warning: "Be careful not to cut the scent gland at the vent, as it has a sickening smell like the boar badger."

The oral history of aboriginal people suggests that they too had a chilly relationship with the wolverine, perhaps even a lingering disdain. One story about the first settlement of the Yukon tells of native people sliding down a steep mountainside, impaling themselves on a sharp stick, and being eaten by the crafty wolverine. Perhaps it is no coincidence that the militant Jones William Ignace, sentenced to fifty-four months in prison for leading a month-long armed standoff at Gustafsen Lake in the British Columbia Interior in 1995, was known to his people and the press simply by his Indian name — Wolverine.

With its bad-ass reputation for strength and durability, the wolverine has become the mascot and corporate symbol for everything from football teams to food processors, workboots to wilderness airlines. Michigan describes itself as the Wolverine State, even though the animal vanished from those parts long ago. Wolverine has also been adopted as the name of a Swedish "death-metal" band, a German punk-rock record label, and a North American mutant comic-book superhero genetically endowed with animal-like senses, razor-sharp extendible claws, and "a berserker rage which he must forever struggle to control."

In truth, the wolverine is nobody's hero, just a rare and fragile species roaming the margins of existence, where it is threatened by the loss of wilderness and the relentless advance of mankind. Although considered the toughest mammal, pound for pound, in the forest, it is no match for bears, cougars, or wolves. Where a wolverine is found feeding on a carcass, it is usually because the larger carnivores have willingly left the kill, not because they were chased away. The wolverine is capable of chewing up even the largest bones with hyena-strength jaws, leaving nothing but white chalk in its scat.

Seldom seen by wilderness travelers, and neglected by science in favor of the big-game animals, it is remarkable that the wolverine has survived at all. Still found in Scandinavia and Eurasia, where the species originally evolved, the wolverine once ranged across North America as far south as New Mexico. Today it has vanished from almost half its historic range and in America's lower 48 states is found in sizeable numbers only in northern Montana. In Canada the species is listed as endangered east of Hudson Bay, where shooting, trapping, and poisoning — some of it aimed at the wolf, on which the wolverine depends for carrion — earlier this century hammered the population into submission. In the west, where the level of human intrusion in wilderness areas is historically not as great, the wolverine is officially listed as vulnerable, a warning sign that western populations, too, could be headed for trouble unless something is done.

That researchers have chosen the Columbia Mountains for their five-year study of the wolverine is no accident. Here among the Interior rainforests, winter conditions strongly favor the unique attributes of the wolverine, offering a place where mythology and science merge to reveal the essence of this elusive animal. The landscape is especially dramatic; mountains drop sharply 6,500 or more feet from alpine peak to valley bottom, with up to half of the annual precipitation falling as snow. Still, the area is very much a rainforest, home to the same western red cedars that thrive on the West Coast. The difference here is that as the snow gradually melts each summer, it provides a continuous water supply to prevent drought, thereby preserving the rainforest ecosystem on the valley bottoms. The area's major community, Revelstoke, a historic railway town of 8,000 residents, receives more precipitation than any other town in the interior of North America — about 950 millimetres (37 inches) annually, December to January being the snowiest months, June and October the rainiest. North of Lake Revelstoke, near Mica Dam, it is even wetter — 1,367 millimetres (54 inches) a year, more precipitation than even soggy Vancouver gets.

The wolverine's feet, well-suited to the heavy snows of the Columbia Mountains, are furry snowshoes that allow the animal to seek out much larger, clumsier game. The landscape is also dominated by avalanche chutes, rivers of white that wind violently down the mountainsides before fanning out into explosive deltas on the valley floor. It is along the base of these chutes that wolverines patrol, using their acute sense of smell and tireless hunting skills to sniff out fallen mountain goats, moose, and deer, then burrowing down with the efficiency of industrial-strength augers as deep as six feet to haul the carcasses out of the snow.

Funding for John Krebs's study comes primarily from the Columbia Basin Fish and Wildlife Compensation Program — guilt money from BC Hydro, which has flooded thousands of acres of prime habitat to create five reservoirs for electricity on the Canadian side of the Columbia River system. The hope is to determine the wolverine's seasonal habitat use and to recommend ways to manage the species in the Interior rainforest. The 7,000-square-kilometre portion of the Columbia Mountains chosen for the study is occupied by about 25 wolverines and reflects the challenge to the wolverine's existence in a resource-based economy. Although virgin wilderness exists in Glacier and Mount Revelstoke national parks, the greater area is denuded not just by hydroelectric dams but by clearcut logging, mining, helicopter skiing, snowmobiling, back-country skiing, railways, traplines, and the Trans-Canada Highway. "When I show photos of the area to the Americans," remarks Krebs, driving along the east shore of Lake Revelstoke, "they wonder how we still have wolverines with habitat like that."

Even under the best of conditions, wolverines suffer from low population densities and a slow reproduction rate. In the Columbia Mountains, males typically occupy overlapping home ranges of 1,000 square kilometres, compared with 300 square kilometres for females. Wolverines may require only half that much territory in national parks, where the natural landscape makes for better habitat. While they prefer to inhabit wilderness areas far from human disturbance, wolverines are known to cross highways and railways and to scavenge roadkills, risky behavior that occasionally results in death. Although they are mostly solitary creatures, wolverines come together to breed between April and October. Pregnancy is delayed in the female until December to March; depending on food resources, she can abort or give birth to two to four kits in late winter to early spring. In 1998 only one of ten radio-collared females successfully reproduced. Rearing the young is also difficult because the female wolverine travels far and wide in search of food.

For researchers, finding their way through the study area is usually more dangerous than any encounter with a wolverine. Logging roads are the main point of access — narrow, slippery, and marked "travel at your own risk" because of the potential for head-on collisions. And then there are the occasions when even a four-wheel-drive truck is insufficient for the job. At one point during our tour, the lanky, affable Krebs parks alongside the Trans-Canada Highway east of Revelstoke and removes a snowmobile from the back of his pickup to check a trap a short distance down a trail. Taking a good run at a bank of snow that has built up on the shoulder of the highway, Krebs becomes airborne as the machine clears the top rim, recoils with a high-pitched squeal, and crashes back to earth with a heavy thud. He leaps to one side, bruising his knee and ripping his snowpants in the process, narrowly avoiding being flattened.

By 1998, Krebs and his colleagues had managed to live-trap thirty-nine wolverines — fourteen females, twenty-five males — in the study area. That's a big improvement from the early days of the research program, when sixteen radio collars went missing in one season, most of them having been slipped off by the wolverines. There is little reduction in circumference from the neck to the head, so researchers have learned the hard way that they must be extremely accurate when fitting collars. Too much slack and the wolverine quickly works it off; too little and it risks a slow suffocation. "Radiocollaring deer and wolf is fairly easy," explains Krebs, whose father, Charles, is a University of British Columbia zoology professor who headed a landmark study of lynx and snowshoe hare in the Yukon. "Bears are tough because they change weight so dramatically. And so is the weasel family because of the shape of their head and their lifestyle — scavenging, digging around rocks, hooking on stuff. They just beat 'em up."

To capture the wolverines, researchers construct coffin-sized live-traps from available timber and set them into the snow. Frozen road-killed deer or elk, supplemented with beaver carcasses from a local trapper, are used as bait. Fetching the rotting carcasses and splitting them like cordwood for the traps is the least enviable part of the job. "I was in to my elbows yesterday, chopping beavers," he laments.

"Disgusting. It stank. But 'That's good,' I have to keep reminding myself."

When the wolverine tugs hard on the heavy bait at the far end of the trap, the heavy log roof falls down and trips a magnetized transmitter beacon, alerting biologists to the capture. Occasionally wind or snow moves the magnet, or an aggressive marten succeeds in setting off the trap, sending frustrated biologists out on a false alarm. But with black and grizzly bears in their winter dens, the wolverine is generally the only animal around that is strong enough to pull the heavy bait and spring the trap. When that happens, biologists waste little time getting to the scene, for wolverines, with their powerful jaws and determination, are capable of chewing their way to freedom through a log the size of a linebacker's calf in a day. "Wolverines are the ultimate opportunists," confirms Krebs. "They never cease to amaze me."

Sixteen live traps are located within the study area — some a short walk from the labyrinth of logging roads intersecting the valley bottoms, others accessible by snowmobile, cross-country skis, or snowshoes, and a few so isolated they require the services of a helicopter. Our destination on this particular afternoon is one such place — the upper Goldstream River, a hundred kilometres due north of Revelstoke. Chartering a Bell 206 helicopter from a heli-skiing operation conveniently located within the lower reaches of the Goldstream River, our flight is a brief fifteen minutes across a green-and-white checkerboard landscape.

That industrial logging has a profound impact on wildlife is evidenced by one particular clearcut, not more than twenty-five acres, occupied by perhaps twenty moose. The thumping roar of the helicopter's rotor must be deafening in the narrow valley bottom, but the moose scarcely even look up. Accustomed by now to the comings and goings of the heli-skiers, these gentle giants continue to graze on the clearcut's young willows and shrubs as placidly as Holsteins. It is an incongruous scene, enough to make one think that clearcutting might be good for wildlife after all. But the unnatural grouping of so many moose in one place must have its drawbacks, too, allowing wolves and human hunters, for that matter, to follow a logging road right to a certain kill. The loss of old-growth forests can also leave moose vulnerable, with nowhere to seek refuge from an especially deep snowfall.

After touching down in the upper valley, we wade through knee-deep drifts to the live-trap at the base of a small hemlock tree. All is quiet inside, not so much as a growl or the clawing of wood, which may come as a surprise to everyone but the researchers. "I've only had two wolverines that were fairly cranky," explains trapping contractor Dave Lewis. "That reputation is a fallacy. Most are pretty docile. Each is an individual, but this one is fairly typical, quiet as a little mouse."

Laying out his drug paraphernalia on the snow, Lewis fills a syringe with the sedative Telozol and attaches it to a metal jabstick. "Okay, we're ready for action," he says, eliciting a low rumbling growl from the wolverine as he carefully raises the roof of the trap and crawls onto his stomach for a better look. Two minutes after Lewis delivers a sharp poke to the wolverine's backside, the drug takes effect, allowing for the speedy removal of the animal, a two-year-old male about the bulk of a medium-sized dog. It is promptly named Lorenzo — the name I assumed during a recent trip to Mexico's Yucatan Peninsula. I am flattered. I think. Secretly I wonder how I will respond if Lorenzo gets schmucked by a train and winds up flatter than a road-kill gopher.

Researchers take his weight and measurements — thirteen kilograms and almost three feet from nose to stubby tail — tag both ears, and fit his neck with a radio collar, a temporary irritant designed to rot off in two years unless researchers are able to recapture him and fit a new one. For Lorenzo, it is siesta time. He sleeps soundly under the effect of the drug, even snores and heaves a couple of big sighs. I cannot resist the opportunity to take a close-up shot standing next to him, the sort of thing you might do if you found Arnold Schwarzenegger passed out in a bar. Lorenzo's most distinctive feature is not his jaws and teeth — formidable as they are when his lips are pressed back — but his thick, warm coat. Dark chocolate in color, with a lighter patch on the backside, the pelt features a thick inner layer of gray fur the consistency of laundry lint, and a luxurious outer layer of long guard hairs. The pelt is among the warmest of those of furbearing animals in North America and was long used by aboriginal people as a fringe for parka headgear because its double layers resist ice-up in winter.

Finished with Lorenzo after just fifteen minutes, the researchers dig a small recovery pit in the snow not far away. The idea is that when the wolverine is capable of climbing out of the pit, it should have recovered enough not to do anything stupid, like wander into the river and drown. As we wait at a distance for Lorenzo to shake off his hangover, there is time to consider some preliminary observations of the ongoing studies. What researchers are finding in the Columbia Mountains is that females typically den far from human activity in roadless, undeveloped drainages, especially in the parks, setting up shop in old avalanche chutes or under woody debris at elevations of about 5,000 feet. The impact of logging remains mixed: wolverines have been observed feeding on wolf-kill carcasses in open clearcuts and traveling along narrow firebreaks between timber stands. But researchers are also concerned that clearcut logging, especially around female den sites, could cause serious disruption, uprooting the wolverines from otherwise suitable habitat at the most critical time.

Another of the key research findings is that wolverines spend less time traveling on barren alpine ridges than in the forest habitat, both the cedar-hemlock and the Engelmann spruce-subalpine fir forests. And in their wide-ranging search for food — it is not unusual for wolverines to cover 20 to 40 kilometres in a day — they become easy targets for trappers. In just one season, one animal traveled at least 200 kilometres, from Bigmouth Creek, where it was radio-collared, to Findlay Creek, where it died in a trap. The jury is still out on whether restrictions are necessary on trapping wolverines. The British Columbia government has not restricted wolverine trapping despite a sharp decline in harvest, from a peak 634 animals in the winter of 1973–74 to as few as 128 in 1996, at an average pelt price of $238. At the same time, in the lower forty-eight states only a handful of wolverines are legally harvested each winter. Researchers such as Krebs know the trapping industry has the potential to threaten populations: three wolverines were trapped one winter in the Goldstream River on just one of ten traplines in the study area.

Eventually Lorenzo begins to stir. Looking like a newborn bear cub, he briefly pokes his nose above the rim of the recovery pit. But he cannot quite climb out; the drug has not yet worked its way out of his hind legs. After several more attempts he manages to scale the walls and strike out on his own. Hesitant at first, he advances a few steps, then whips quickly around to see if anyone . . . anything is following him. He does not detect us, does not even look in our direction. Instead he lopes steadily uphill, with the distinctive bouncing gait of a weasel or river otter, weaves through a patch of snow-covered clearcut stumps, and melts into a thick patch of old-growth forest.

Will the future of the wolverine in British Columbia also be an uphill struggle, waged against shrinking wilderness and the endless demands of a growing human population? Krebs often ponders the question. "If we can keep the prey around and work on limiting access, if we can manage ourselves and our own activities — both the trapping harvest and logging, especially around denning time — I think we can keep wolverines without having to make the whole Columbia Mountains into a park. But wolverines exist in a very marginal niche . . . and our options are dwindling fast."

—

In the months after Lorenzo left my view, he continued to fill my thoughts: I wondered how he might fare against the minefield of natural and human challenges that lay ahead. And, sure enough, less than a year after my visit, Krebs phoned me to deliver the bad news: an inactive signal from Lorenzo's transmitter led researchers to his carcass in mountainous terrain south of Revelstoke. He had died in a fight, they concluded, either lanced by a mountain goat's sharp black daggers or raked and chewed apart by the rainforest's most efficient and stealthful predator, the cougar. Either way, I took solace in knowing Lorenzo hadn't suffered the indignity of being squished by an eighteen-wheel transport truck or sliced in two by a freight train. He died naturally, which is the most a wolverine can hope for in the shrinking wilderness of the Columbia Mountains.

CHAPTER 4

# The Cruelest Cut

*The Tlingits of*
*Southeast Alaska*

CHARLES JACK JR. hasn't been in Mary's Cafe for five minutes, but he's managed to strike up a conversation with every customer, employee, and stranger in the joint. His cousin, a trash collector, complains that residents are trying to break his back by filling their garbage cans with heavy cockleshells. The waitress unloads about the ravenous brown bear that wandered into her backyard and ate her barbecue — a $250 sandwich, just two months old. One story leads to another, and before you know it, everyone is complaining about all those outsiders who've come to Hoonah over the years to hunt the small but tasty Sitka black-tailed deer and wind up lowering the bag limits for the locals. Eventually Jack looks out the window at the dirty old freighter, *Pan Leader*, home port Inchon, South Korea, loading raw logs in Port Frederick. Then he screws up his face, as though he just found a fly in his coffee, turns to me at the next table, and volunteers, "That's quite a rust bucket out there, isn't it? Worst I've ever seen."

Mary's is the social and culinary hub of Hoonah, a remote community of 1,000 people, 80 percent of them Tlingit natives, on Chichagof Island in the Alaska Panhandle. The cafe stands tippy-toe on wooden stilts on the waterfront and, like most places in town, enjoys a commanding view of Port Frederick. There is no sign outside the cafe and no need for one. Mary's is the only restaurant on Front Street, known not so much for great food as savory conversation. And one topic served up most every day is logging and the way it has ruined everyone's view. Not logging done by some faceless multinational corporation, mind you, but logging by the natives themselves. Logging that has despoiled the very landscape onto which residents must cast their eyes every day of their lives.

A straight-line distance of three miles across the waters of Port Frederick sprawl the desolate hills of West Port. No one lives there. No humans, anyway. And not much else by the look of things. Clearcutting approved by the Huna Totem Corporation has pretty much obliterated West Port. Timeless rainforests are now a rogue clearcut that begins at one end and just keeps on going, sparing only a few patches of trees on top, a few more trees spilling vertically down both sides of the creeks, and a narrow scruffy fringe along the beachfront. The old growth is gone, ripped asunder, never to be seen again by anyone living today in Hoonah. Nor by anyone's children or grandchildren, for that matter. Even if future generations choose to preserve rather than log again, which is an overly optimistic hope, it would take 250 years to restore West Port to some semblance of a mature temperate rainforest. And it's anyone's guess how many species of, say, fungi or insects unique to that particular patch of old growth would be lost forever in the process.

Every community is responsible for drawing its line in the sand between development and preservation, between profit and lifestyle. For Hoonah's residents, the line washed out with the tide. And West Port is the messy result. What happened here is tantamount to clear-cutting Vancouver's postcard backdrop, Grouse Mountain, or the lower slopes of Washington state's natural icon, Mount Rainier. No, the people of Hoonah are not proud of what happened. Most are disgusted by it. But Jack, sixty-two and the eldest of ten children, is one of the few honest enough to say he likes the cash — the corporate dividends he receives from the native logging of Chichagof Island — and is secure in knowing the forest shall someday return, if only as a second-growth mockup. Watching the decaying *Pan Leader* grow heavy with its booty of aboriginal heritage, he remarks, "Those who complain about the eyesore don't understand. They don't realize there will be logs for their grandchildren."

For Hoonah, the sad road to industrial devastation began with the United States government's passage of the Alaska Native Claims Settlement Act of 1971. The legislation was meant not just to resolve long-standing native claims to Alaskan soil, but to bring aboriginal people into the capitalist fold, to once and for all replace the proud traditions of the hunter-gatherer with the mercenary values of corporate America. From that perspective, it worked. With a steady flow of cash dividends, natives have become more reliant on supermarkets than on traditional hunting, fishing, and trapping. At the corporate level, they have proven that greed knows no ethnic boundaries, no color but green. "When you give people that much control and money without experience, there are a lot of pitfalls," Jack continues, washing down the unappetizing conclusion with another coffee. "It doesn't matter what you do, it all comes down to how much money you can put in your pocket, same as any corporation anywhere else."

Under the 1971 settlement, Huna Totem Corporation received

title to 23,000 acres around Hoonah, although it took about a decade to gain legal possession of those lands. The regional mother corporation — Juneau-based Sealaska, of which Huna is one of a dozen members — got another 400,000 acres, 11 percent of which are located around Hoonah. Since then, much has changed. Huna Totem concluded it was better suited to the investment business than to clearcut logging. In two sales, in 1994 and 1995, Huna granted Sealaska the stumpage rights to its remaining timber lands from the 1971 settlement — decisions that led directly to the razing of West Port and to the creation of clearcuts so vast that even Sealaska officials don't know their size. "I don't know that I've ever gone out and said, 'How big is a clearcut?'" said Sealaska's senior vice-president of resources, Rick Harris, a fish scientist by training. "There's about 8,000 acres of clearcuts there on Sealaska lands. When does one clearcut end and another begin? There is no limit, per se, none of those type of restrictions on a harvest."

He is right, tragic as it may be. Because logging on native land is governed by Alaska state law, native corporations are exempt from tough new regulations being implemented on neighboring lands in the Tongass National Forest, at almost seventeen million acres the largest national forest in the United States. A sweeping land-management plan adopted for the Tongass in 1997 accepts as a basic tenet that 70 percent of the forest's more than 300 wildlife species are reliant on old-growth stands. As such, the plan dictates that logging not encroach within 1,000 feet of an estuary or beachfront to minimize disturbance to nesting bald eagles, America's proud symbol; that one million acres be protected as old-growth reserves; that clearcuts be reduced to an average of just thirty acres; that a minimum 100-foot riparian buffer be preserved on either side of fish-bearing streams; and that the average annual harvest be cut in half, with an emphasis on allowing forests to mature to 100 years before harvest.

In comparison, the Alaska Forest Resources and Practices Act gives new meaning to the phrase "The Last Frontier." Under state legislation pertaining to private lands there is no ban on the export of raw unprocessed logs, no restriction on the size of clearcuts, no requirement for buffers along beaches, and no regulations for the protection of wildlife habitat. Essentially, all Sealaska is legally required to do is maintain a twenty-yard riparian buffer on each side of fish-bearing streams — something it has had trouble doing. In August 1996 the state fined Sealaska $7,500 for logging inside the riparian buffer in a drainage south of Hoonah. Although the contractor — Whitestone Logging, a non-native Alaskan company based at Hoonah — was fingered for much of the blame, Sealaska was held ultimately responsible for the project and for failing to exercise due diligence.

To hear Harris tell it, Sealaska has gone the extra distance for the environment at West Port, voluntarily leaving a series of vertical corridors for deer migration and a 100-foot beachfront buffer. As well, and despite all appearances to the contrary, Sealaska has only exercised about half its cutting rights on West Port. "Totem made a business decision to sell the timber," Harris is quick to add. "If someone else had bought it, they would have gone through it as quickly as possible to recover their investment as quickly as possible."

Alaska's Tlingits are an example of just how far coastal natives have strayed from their ancestors' traditional use of the forests. Using stone, bone, wood, and shell implements, later replaced by steel after the arrival of Europeans and Russians, aboriginal people were adept at putting wood to work. Western red cedar — light, durable, and functional — met the core of their needs, including kindling for fires, mats, ceremonial bowls, dug-out canoes, and longhouses. The bark of western hemlock was used for tanning and dyeing; the wood for spoons, feast bowls, spear shafts, and halibut hooks; and the branches for bedding, skirts, and headdresses, as well as for collecting herring roe. The inner bark of Sitka spruce was dried into cakes or eaten with berries; the roots were made into hats and baskets; the sharp needles were used in boughs for ceremonial dances to ward off evil. The buds and leaves of black cottonwood were used for treating pain and rheumatism, the young shoots for sweatlodge frames, the roots for fishtraps, and the wood for smoking fish. Pine pitch was made into glue, waterproofing, scents, and medicines. The strong branches of the western yew were used for paddles, digging sticks, adze handles, clubs, and wedges. The bark of yellow cedar was used for whaling rope; its wood for dishes, chests, and masks; and its boughs were used to make fishing-net hoops.

But that rich cultural link appears severed and bleeding today in Hoonah. How did it happen? How could people with such a long-standing connection to the land have done such a thing? To find some answers I seek out Albert Dick, the mayor of Hoonah and chair of the Huna Totem Corp. I find him shoehorned into his modest office in the single-story city hall across the street from Mary's Cafe. He is a burly man in the West Coast native tradition, with an equally big smile. When he talks, he leans way over on his desk, like an old-growth spruce swaying in the wind. "We're all logged out," he confirms flatly. "We sold all we had left to Sealaska. We're all done. We have no more trees to sell." Money from the logging has been pumped back into corporation investments — stocks and bonds, even a shopping centre in Everett, Washington. In return, natives get their regular dividends — guilt money, some would say. In 1971, tribal members each got 100 shares in Huna Totem, which Dick says now yield a quarterly investment dividend of about US$1,000, plus another $1,200 from a special $38 million settlement trust fund. You can't buy or sell the shares, but you can bequeath them to another person. Charles Jack Jr., for example, holds 400 shares. The Sealaska dividend is modest, about $300 a year for each of the 16,000 natives who belong to the dozen member corporations. All tallied, it's not a lot of money — less than $10,000 a year for a 100-share investment — but it's a steady income, and shareholders come to rely on it. Asked if the overall effect of the 1971 settlement has been good or bad for Alaskan natives, Dick is quick to respond, "Probably bad. We seem to be getting away from our culture. Our traditional values are disappearing. In the old days, our families were closer. We've gotten spoiled."

Nobody's role has changed more drastically than that of the native politician, now under pressure to make money, to keep the dividends rolling in or risk getting turfed at the next election. "There is pressure," Dick agrees, sweat pouring down his forehead. "Our job is to make money. The nature of people is they always want more."

For another perspective I seek out the U.S. Forest Service office in Hoonah, a fifteen-minute walk east of town along the waterfront. Here I find that logging cutbacks on federal lands have generated a bunker mentality among employees like Tim Hazlewood, distinguished by a camouflage hat as he toils away in his darkened rear office. "We're more than under siege," says the timber management assistant. "We're just about dead."

As a result of logging cutbacks on Tongass lands in southeast Alaska, the Alaska Forest Association estimates the number of direct timber jobs has declined since 1990 by 3,000 workers to just 1,600. The three biggest mills shut down: the Alaska Pulp Corporation's pulp mills in Sitka and its associated sawmill in Wrangell, and Louisiana Pacific's Ketchikan Pulp Company operation. No one expects a return to the logging heydays that followed the opening of southeast Alaska's first big mill, Ketchikan Pulp, in 1954, and the Sitka mill in 1959. In fact, the industry's only glimmer of hope is negotiations between Louisiana Pacific and Sealaska over the possible joint development of a laminated-veneer lumber plant on the old Ketchikan Pulp site.

Hazlewood recently conducted his own survey of the approximately 900 federal employees in the Tongass forest and estimated that no more than 40 are directly employed in the field on harvesting operations. "In the past, we tried to keep the mills going, that was our job," Hazlewood says. "We haven't cut a tree here since 1995, just blow-down salvage."

But even industry supporters know logging must have its limits. Hazlewood too has problems with the style and volume of harvesting on the native corporation lands around Hoonah. Now that most of the timber is gone, he hopes some good comes of it — if not for the forests, for the people. "They are managing to make money on the rapid removal of the timber. Hopefully they will use it wisely for the long-term betterment of the community." As a non-native Hoonah resident who does not enjoy the income of a dividend cheque, he admits to the dissatisfaction of having to look at the mess out there on West Port every day. "The biggest impact is on the people looking at it right across town. Everybody in the world sees it. People really don't like it." Although the native logging has resulted in displacement of wildlife and an eyesore for residents, Hazlewood notes that the forests are quick to regenerate on their own here on the rain-soaked coast. In fact, natural regeneration is the norm throughout southeast Alaska, where foresters rely on the natural healing powers of climate and rainfall. "Regeneration is prolific, 3,000 to 6,000 trees per acre," he asserts. "God had caulk boots when he made this country."

On the walk back to town I begin to appreciate what a nice little place Hoonah is, despite the lingering smell of corporation politics. I have been to towns so small and geographically remote that locals sit in starling formation at the lunch counter discussing the weather report and watching tourists as though they were two-headed spring calves. Or small towns in which the residents' rude sense of curiosity is replaced by impersonal disdain. For instance, a waitress in Valdez,

Alaska, at the time of the *Exxon Valdez* oil tanker spill in 1989, made me open a bottle of wine myself by giving me an opener that, honest to God, still held the cork from the last customer.

Hoonah is not like those places. People here are genuinely friendly, open, and welcoming — one trait of aboriginal culture that lives on. Pedestrians say hello and motorists wave, even though they haven't the slightest clue who I am. And then there are those people who are in a league of their own when it comes to hospitality. People like Presbyterian church pastor Greg Howald and his wife, Carol, a couple who've turned glad-handing into a career. When Charles Jack Jr. heard I was planning to stay overnight at the church, he told me about the time the Howalds overheard his wife lament that she couldn't afford the half-hour flight to Juneau. The couple responded by dropping by unannounced with a free airline ticket and spending cash to boot.

I had been advised to stay at the Presbyterian church during my visit to Hoonah, holing up in the basement for a small donation rather than forking out sixty dollars for the town's only motel, a dingy operation located inconveniently out of town. Why not? The Presbyterians are a middle-of-the-road Protestant denomination that does not practice overt evangelism, and the Howalds aren't the type to ask for your religious credentials at the door. In true Christian tradition they accept all equally, no questions asked. When I show up unannounced on their doorstep with my hulking backpack, I am waved inside with all the affection given to a long-lost friend. Ordering me to leave on my shoes, the pastor asks, "Who'd put white carpet in a house in southeast Alaska?" He shows me the clothes washer and dryer on the main floor of their house, and the phone on the kitchen counter. "Use 'em as required," he says, adding I shouldn't knock next time. Just walk in and make myself at home. "Don't sweat the small stuff," he says. Oh yeah. One more thing: if I'm interested, moose-loaf dinner is served at 6:15 p.m., and if I really insist on bringing something, which I do, how about ice cream?

My sleeping quarters are in the church basement, a perspective that guarantees a view of Christianity from the ground floor up. I roll out my inflatable mat and sleeping bag on the blue carpet next to a Sunday school banner that reads "Jesus sets me free." Then I rest my bulky backpack up against an old green pew that is serving a stint as an ordinary bench. There are no curtains over the basement windows, and every so often a few kids press their faces against the glass to check me out. "Put away your valuables," suggests a young seminary student who is visiting from Seattle and staying in a room just down the hall. "Sometimes the young children come in here. You never know."

The Presbyterians first established a mission in Hoonah in 1881, but that building burned down in 1944, along with the rest of the town, in a violent conflagration sparked by a native salmon-smoking operation. The replacement church, completed two years later, remains a prominent white building on the waterfront but is only one of several churches in town. There are the Catholics, the Pentecostals, and, of course, the Russian Orthodox, a relic from the historic Russian presence in southeast Alaska, dating back more than 250 years, long before America's purchase of Alaska for $7.2 million in 1867.

A native of Indiana, Greg came to southeast Alaska in 1976 with the United States Coast Guard and later moved into policing. He served seven years, the last two as police chief, in the native community of Kake, population 1,200, on neighboring Admiralty Island. A longtime churchgoer with no theological education, he found policing in a small native community the closest thing to pastoring. "I wanted to do something to try to help people," he says. "Policing is more personal in a small native community where everyone is related. Here, you wind up being a social worker."

As Greg witnessed a disturbingly high turnover rate among pastors not committed to the remote village lifestyle — "They come and go, like flowing water" — he agreed to be trained by the Presbyterian church to take on the job himself. After four years in Hoonah, he can figure on a congregation of forty on a typical Sunday, if such a thing exists in rural Alaska, where routines are largely governed by hunting and fishing seasons. Part of Greg's philosophy is to meld native spirituality with Christianity whenever he can get away with it. "The Tlingits have always believed in a heavenly creator, have always prayed to God," he says. "There are a lot of parallels a fellow can play with." He likes to compare the twelve tribes of ancient Israel to, coincidentally, the twelve tribes of the Tlingit nation. "The Israelites were hunter-gatherer people, traveling from place to place, gathering their food in season. Same thing that these people do."

Carol Howald is something of a rarity: although born in Tacoma, she has lived in southeast Alaska since age two. That puts her in a good position to view the changes brought on by logging. She laments the way the native corporations have logged Hoonah, saying that if it had been done gradually, it might have provided longer-term employment while protecting wildlife habitat. "Some areas of southeast Alaska look like Ireland. The trees have gone." As for the human implications of the 1971 native land claim settlement, she feels it has only compounded the difficulties. "The alcohol, the social problems — it's gotten a lot worse."

There are two liquor outlets on Front Street. The private liquor store is distinguished by a sign outside reading "Corona Street" and by the queue of customers that starts forming shortly before the door opens at 1 p.m. And then there's the tavern, one of those industrial-strength places where you could drop, throw, or kick pretty much anything and nobody would notice the difference. I walk inside for a quick peek, but the place is uncomfortably quiet. A middle-aged white man watches television at one end of the bar, while an elderly native man sits at the other end, playing crib with the bartender, a white woman in her thirties.

"I need a name for my pet cat," she remarks.

"Why don't you call it the Tlingit word for cat? Douche," he replies, straight-faced.

To which she erupts, "I can't call it that! What will my white neighbors think if I run outside and shout, 'Here Douche, here Douche'?"

Despite the colorful bar conversation, I find the town itself more interesting, a curious hodgepodge of simple wood-frame homes erected since the 1944 fire. In sharp contrast to the cruise-ship towns on the Panhandle, Hoonah has no tourist shops, not so much as a postcard. But visitors find more than enough curiosities to keep them busy. Dixie's Espresso, a makeshift outlet, is especially popular in the mornings. There is the big black dog with a guilty look running down Front Street, dragging ten yards of rope behind him. The pay phone drips graffiti reading "I peed on this." And there is the bingo pull-tab parlor, where many of the dividend cheques get cashed. "I have a limit of twenty dollars," insists Cindy Kaze, the clerk at the Wings of Alaska airline office. "People just keep spending and spending. I don't know how they do it."

There is no movie theatre in town, but court sits weekdays in a small room out back of city hall, and that can be just as entertaining and a whole lot more informative. Proceedings are already in session when I walk in — the only person in court who isn't paid or ordered to be here — and sit down on a plastic assembly-hall chair. State district magistrate Joyce Skaflestad presides, with the American flag on her right, the Alaskan flag on her left. Speaking over the loud growl of a chainsaw on the waterfront, she sentences a man to a fifty dollar fine and one year's probation for violating state fish-and-game laws by using bait on his line. Then she returns to her office, just outside, to await the next case.

I follow her out, killing time by reading the lobby bulletin board, when she walks up confidently in her black robes and asks if I need any assistance. She catches me off guard. This sort of thing does not happen in Vancouver, where judges stay as far away from journalists as possible, and where I have even struggled with judicial secretaries for the full names behind their bosses' initials. Now I have a judge walk up and ask if there's anything she can do for me. Well, okay, what about those clearcuts outside? What's your verdict on them? To my surprise, she proceeds to tell me. A resident of Hoonah for thirty years, Skaflestad compares the native corporations to students who have advanced two grades in school and are now playing catch-up on their learning. She is especially annoyed at the insensitive tactics adopted by Sealaska to justify boosting its profit margins: the corporation even planned to clearcut Hoonah's watershed until protests stopped it. "They can talk all they want about preserving native traditions, but it is a corporation for profit."

Skaflestad walks a fine line in Hoonah. She knows virtually everyone who comes before her in court, information she must put aside during their trial. "I can sleep at night," she says. By the same token, she makes a point of not judging people on the street by what happened in her courtroom. Before heading back to court to sentence three teenaged girls for drinking in public under the legal age of twenty-one, she expresses concern that social problems may increase as the community struggles into the twenty-first century. Too much has been logged too quickly. With governments tightening up the welfare laws and the fishing industry employing fewer fishers all the time, there will be repercussions when the logging jobs run out. "The community hasn't planned for anything else," she says, noting that the "terrible" clearcuts around town have killed any potential for tourism. "It will come as a shock. I don't know what it will do to the community."

As Skaflestad is called back into court, I wander down to the waterfront for one last look at the big ecological sinkhole swallowing up the West Port skyline. Who knows? Maybe Hoonah residents got what they deserved — a taste of frontier justice. But I have to wonder what Mother Nature did to deserve this sentence. Propping myself up against a rock on the beach, I run my eyes along the disheveled Hoonah shoreline. A busted-up wooden boat, an outboard motor, and a near-new mountain bike rock back and forth in the waves at high tide — evidence of a people who have ignored the wisdom of their ancestors, and forgotten to appreciate not just what they have, but what they stand to lose. And, just offshore, the final insult: the *Pan Leader*, sitting low in the water, its belly bloated with Alaska's oldest rainforests, ready to sail away with its share of Tlingit pride.

# CHAPTER 5

# Through the Eyes
# of the *Nitinat Chief*
### *Logging British Columbia's*
### *Central Coast*

NITINAT LAKE WOULD not be my first choice for a canoe trip. The place conveys the distinct impression that it has given up the fight, lost the will to live, and that any industrial activity still found around here is almost certainly in the mop-up stage. The evidence is everywhere to see: a mange of ragged clearcuts creeping across the mountainous terrain; the soil weeping one landslide after another, a result of gravel roads hacked into the steep slopes; a logging truck, bloated with profit, waddling to a log sort; and a helicopter-logging operation transforming the last few patches of green forest into unsightly brown ant hills.

But here I am anyway, like a nuclear-holocaust survivor paddling toward the Pacific Ocean, taking inventory of the destruction and shaking my head at how it all might have begun. The *Nitinat Chief* could speak volumes on the subject. The wooden tugboat is a child of the rainforest, built in 1941 specifically to haul old-growth logs from the shores of Nitinat Lake, on the west coast of Vancouver Island, out to the Pacific en route to the region's lumber mills. If only it had been that easy. To accomplish its singular task the *Nitinat Chief* faced one of the most daunting routes on the coast, a harrowing run through the gauntlet of Nitinat Narrows, a navigational bottleneck known to modern mariners simply as The Gap. Depending on the tides, water from the lake either hurtles through the bottleneck and into the open ocean, or the ocean's unbridled surf bashes its way back into the lake. Either way, the clash of wills can be a violent one. To be caught in The Gap at the wrong hour on the wrong day is to ride a writhing cobra, hanging on for dear life as it rises back on itself for one last hiss against the mongoose of the Pacific.

Bob Lea knows. He has stared down the beast. He has seen Nitinat Narrows at its worst during a logging career that spanned fifty years, beginning as deckhand, mate, and engineer alongside the *Nitinat Chief.* Now seventy-seven and holed up in the Vancouver Island retirement community of Ladysmith, Lea still recalls with a shudder the task of repeatedly hauling two log rafts — each twenty yards wide and forty yards long — through the narrows. "Go through too fast and you couldn't steer, and the logs would hit the rocks," he explains, stopping briefly to gather his breath. "It's one of the worst places in the world, no question about it."

Engineers designed the *Nitinat Chief* to meet the challenges of Nitinat Narrows. The boat is a burly seventy feet long, with a draft to skim over the shallow bars, and is crafted from some of Vancouver Island's sturdiest Douglas firs. It is driven by a four-cylinder, 160-horsepower engine salvaged from the *Varsity*, a sixty-five-foot halibut boat that crashed onto the rocks and sank just a short way up the coast. But even after the logging industry doubled the width of The

Gap to fifty yards in an ambitious blasting program, the place continued to pose a potentially lethal hazard. Skippers were known to tie up for a week or more alongside a cannery in the approach to The Gap, just inside Nitinat Lake, waiting for the weather to improve.

When conditions allowed, the *Nitinat Chief* would squeeze through at slack tide or on a high-water ebb, when the lake's outflow gave the tug an edge. The return trip proved just as tricky: as the tug entered The Gap, it risked being sucker-punched from behind by the unpredictable ocean swells. A big wave could hoist the stern clear of the water, plunge the bow nose first into the surf, and spin the entire tug dangerously around end to end. Lea recalls one trip during which the tug lunged sideways so violently that a box of coal used for the galley stove, along with a set of gas cans, rocketed overboard. Lost forever. "I remember having to go around the beaches picking up bark for cooking," he says with a lingering smile. "We did that until we got to town."

Industrial logging at Nitinat Lake was a brutish pursuit in those early days of the Second World War. British Columbia's rainforests did their part to help fuel the Allies' military machine, providing, among other things, a supply of Sitka spruce for the construction of the wooden frames of the famous Mosquito bomber aircraft. Power saws were still in their infancy, too big and heavy and unreliable to replace the axe, the crosscut saw, and the dependable immigrant as the method of choice for felling timber. The steamy smell of oxen teams at work had long evaporated from the woods, but coastal railway logging operations were in their heyday. And timber was hauled out of the bush on a high-lead cable system that employed a spar tree — often a standing Douglas fir, its limbs and top sawed off by a fearless, axe-wielding logger equipped with spurs — and a complex assortment of blocks, swivels, and wire ropes powered by a gas or diesel donkey engine.

Even the transport of logs by water had a different look in those days. Rather than employ a typical flat boom that might break up in bad weather, with the ensuing loss of valuable timber, logging companies on the storm-battered Pacific coast built big Davis rafts. They were the 1911 invention of a Canadian, G.G. Davis, superintendent at the British Canadian Lumber Company camp at Port Renfrew on the west coast of Vancouver Island. One raft consisted of a base of logs strapped together, figure-eight style, with thick wire rope. Succeeding layers hoisted on top contained two logs fewer than the last, and a raft contained as many as seven or eight layers. The rafts were especially well adapted to the exposed waters of Juan de Fuca Strait, the international waterway that funnels oceangoing freighters to or from the protected, populated waters of Washington's Puget Sound and British Columbia's Strait of Georgia. So impervious were these rafts to storms that one lost at sea was sighted several weeks later, intact, floating 5,000 kilometres away in the North Pacific.

These days the *Nitinat Chief* and the Davis rafts are ghostly memories on twenty-five-kilometre-long Nitinat Lake. Modern visitors are apt to run up against a much stranger, faster style of craft. Windsurfers. Not just one or two, but hundreds of them, their colorful butterfly wings fluttering in the wind on warm summer days. With its predictable afternoon breezes — a product of the warm land drawing cool air off the Pacific — Nitinat Lake has become Vancouver Island's premier destination for windsurfers. In late July as many as 500 enthusiasts flock to an annual event called Wired, overwhelming the available campsites and surprising anyone innocently navigating up the lake from the Pacific. Canadian Coast Guard hovercraft captain John McGrath recalls threading The Gap en route to sign a series of contracts with native bands located on the lake, to get their assistance with clean-up operations in the event of a marine oil spill. "I thought, 'This is great, we're in the middle of nowhere.' Then we came around the corner and I saw 200 windsurfers scooting around."

Despite the visual atrocities greeting them on the surrounding slopes, canoeists, too, are attracted here in abundance. They launch at the Knob Point forest recreation site on the northwest side of the lake and work their way down the shoreline to the mouth of Hobiton Creek, the entrance to a famous canoe route known as the Nitinat Triangle. This landscape may have a face that could launch a thousand environmental campaigns, but one campaign dominates all others. It is here that British Columbia conservationists cut their teeth in 1970, waging an ultimately successful battle against the Social Credit government's decision to allow British Columbia Forest Products to clearcut the watershed's vast stands of old-growth timber. In a historic decision all but forgotten in today's rancorous political climate, Canada's future prime minister, Jean Chretien, waded into the controversy to support conservation as minister of national parks. Ric Careless, then a neophyte activist helping to lead the preservation fight, vividly remembers Chretien's surprise announcement at a packed public meeting in Victoria. "The crowd exploded into cheering, and the minister's aides were stunned," Careless recalls. "Obviously, the announcement hadn't been part of the intended speech."

Today the Nitinat Triangle connects with Canada's eco poster child, the West Coast Trail, running 77 kilometres from Port Renfrew north to Bamfield. Both the triangle and the trail are part of 125,000-acre Pacific Rim National Park Reserve. Although the West Coast Trail has undergone considerable improvements over the years with the addition of boardwalks, suspension bridges, and organized campsites, the grueling one-hour portage from Nitinat Lake to Hobiton Lake remains as wild and woolly as ever. Canoeists are forced to stagger up steep, unkempt trails, wade through knee-deep bogs, stumble over slippery exposed roots, wag the tail of their canoe through brush to negotiate 90-degree turns, and occasionally lock horns with a rogue hemlock or red cedar blocking the route. Those who survive the weight of the canoe mercilessly bearing down on them seem half an inch shorter than when they started. "At first I was afraid I'd die," offered one war-weary adventurer, Vancouver internal medicine specialist Dr. Bob Rangno. "Then I was afraid I wouldn't." For those who dare, an even tougher hour-and-a-half portage awaits, linking Hobiton to Tsusiat Lake and eventually to the West Coast Trail at Tsusiat Falls, a return circuit usually accomplished in no less than three days.

The other way to reach the West Coast Trail is to bypass the portage to Hobiton Lake altogether, keep paddling down Nitinat Lake, and pull ashore just before the bubbling, tumultuous abyss of Nitinat Narrows. And that is precisely where I am headed with my 27-year-old nephew, Brian, on this overcast September afternoon, fighting a light headwind and sluggish flood tide and keeping to the west shoreline for safety. Although the water is brackish, we spot starfish, sea-nettle jellyfish, and sea sac kelp just beneath our canoe, evidence that Nitinat Lake is more of an ocean inlet than a freshwater lake. This late in the season there are no windsurfers and no other canoeists. Just big chinook salmon leaping from the water three, four, five times — a wake-up call to a line of harbor seals periscoping the surface with their glistening gray heads and moist dark eyes.

By late afternoon we pass a natural formation described on our topographic map as Limestone Bluffs. It is a modest outcrop, but it hints at a much larger natural feature: the hundreds of caves that honeycomb the geologic bedrock of Vancouver Island. Ironically, almost 30 years after conservationists fought to preserve the above-surface beauty of this region, they remain largely ignorant of the diamond just below the surface, one that remains equally vulnerable to siltation and a build-up of wood debris resulting from the clearcutting of the rainforest.

A short paddle west of the bluffs sprawls Mud Bay, a shallow depression of water rich with eelgrass and smug Dungeness crabs that look up and seem to sneer as we pass over them. Farther ahead is added testimony to the productivity of this place: dozens of common mergansers nervously monitor our approach, then rise skyward, one by one, in shotgun formation, producing a hail of beating, overlaid wings. As the flock carves a ragged circle in the sky, it stays well away from three aboriginal men in an aluminum skiff setting fire to a tangle of driftwood and checking crab pots. One fisherman looks up at our passing, makes an up-and-down waving motion with his hand, and asks, "You guys going all the way?" No, we reply. We are traveling to the lip of destruction, just close enough for a look, but no farther. The Gap is no place for a canoe.

As we pass Mud Bay and wend our way to The Gap, even our measured goal seems in jeopardy. The current builds, becomes erratic, pushy. Paddling is a test of strength, tantamount to grabbing the tail of a large wriggling salmon. We hug the corrugated shoreline, passing a crab trap eerily suspended from the mossy limb of a red alder tree, before slowly making our way to a small dock at Whyac. The small settlement is dominated by JR's Grill, a quirky little place that serves as a hangout for Nuu-chah-nulth natives from Vancouver Island to shoot the breeze with their cross-border relatives, the whale-hunting Makah, from Neah Bay, across Juan de Fuca Strait in Washington state. JR's is also a culinary oasis for food-deprived hikers on the West Coast Trail. It represents something of a historic twist — here, natives profit from selling liquor to the Europeans, cans of beer at three dollars a crack.

The trail has become so congested, so popular, that Parks Canada has limited the number of hikers in summer to just fifty-two a day, while exacting a supply-and-demand wilderness tax of seventy dollars per head plus a twenty-five dollar reservation fee. As a result, I have long pooh-poohed the place as a tourist ghetto clogged with foreigners from Europe and America and Australia all reading the same back-packer guidebooks. Why would anyone come here when there is a virtually endless wilderness elsewhere in British Columbia, most of it uninhabited, unexplored, and untaxed?

This position has been an ignorant one, I am about to discover. After only a few dozen steps along the boardwalk leading into the rainforest, I am sold on the place. Incubated by year-round mild temperatures and record rainfall — Henderson Lake, just around the corner, set the North American record in 1997 for annual rainfall at 8.9 metres, or 349 inches — the place sprouts massive trees. In fact, just a day's hike and a watershed away from Nitinat Lake stands the world's tallest Sitka spruce, the Carmanah Giant, which at 310 feet is taller than most apartment buildings and predates Christopher Columbus's arrival in America. Age, unfortunately, does not guarantee respect: to prevent visitors from trampling the Carmanah Giant's life-giving root system into pulp, and to block uncontrolled access to the West Coast Trail, park officials have banned the public from the site.

Our goal today is not a walk in the park, but a first-hand look at Nitinat Narrows. Getting there is a matter of bushwhacking our way through soggy patches of skunk cabbage, scrambling down a steep gully while clinging to salal bushes, and finally emerging at a small stretch of exposed shoreline. And there it is. The Gap. To our left, the restless tongue of Nitinat Lake reaches hungrily toward the Pacific. To our right, the open surf explodes against the rocky outcrops with the shatter of white ice. The scene is drenched in chaos: the current flows through the channel with river force, complete with powerful stretches of white water and swirling, unpredictable eddies. And in the middle of it all, a lone harbor seal spins as precariously as a bug about to be sucked down the bathtub drain.

Inexperienced and overconfident boaters can be sucked down, too, if they misjudge the ferocity of an ocean swell bearing down on them. "There is potential for big trouble," confirms Andy Howell, officer in charge of the Canadian Coast Guard's Bamfield lifeboat station. "There is a lot of current coming out of there, and it's a very narrow spot. If you get a rising tide, with a big sea coming in, you can get standing waves of six, seven feet high. It can be a real danger, a really hairy spot."

In 1994, a forty-five-year-old father and his eighteen-year-old son, Lauren and Jason Holman, were out salmon fishing on Nitinat Lake. Despite high waves at The Gap, they pushed through on a strong ebb tide in their pleasure craft, confronting headlong the horrific wall of water. Tossed into the icy waters and pushed head down into the surf, they faced almost certain drowning if not for the heroic efforts of two other fishermen, Tom Walton and Ken MacDowell. Where other potential rescuers dared not venture that day, these two men risked their lives to maneuver their own craft through the swells to pluck the bloodied and exhausted Holmans from the ocean. For their efforts, Walton and MacDowell were recognized as heroes one year later and awarded the Royal Life Saving Society's Medal of Bravery.

Standing safely on this little patch of beach, I can appreciate that the concoction of current and rocks and surf is as volatile today as it was during the heyday of the *Nitinat Chief.* But that knowledge only satisfies half my curiosity about the early days of logging on British Columbia's battered coastline. I am equally interested in the fate of the tug itself, a witness to so many changes in the temperate rainforest. To find the answers, however, I must look beyond this notorious stretch of coastline known as the "Graveyard of the Pacific," beyond the farthest reaches of Vancouver Island, to a mysterious and secret place tucked deep in the belly folds of central British Columbia, 500 kilometres to the north.

As the reincarnated *Nitinat Chief* gently noses its way out of Bella Coola harbor on its way to the latest clash between environmentalists and loggers in the war of the woods, it occurs to me that few soldiers have seen more action on the western rainforest front. By the time businessman Brad Widsten became the *Nitinat Chief*'s fourth owner, buying her for $80,000 in 1987, the tug had towed not just Davis rafts but modern log booms, coal, and wood chips. It had even served a stint as a live-aboard vessel for a small-scale logging operation.

For all its weary sojourns up and down the coast, the *Chief* is in prime shape. When Widsten bought the old tug, he decided to preserve it not just as a priceless piece of maritime history, but to turn a profit in the changing world of industrial forestry. He invested more than $200,000 on an extensive overhaul that included new caulking, a fresh skin of protective gumwood sheathing on the hull, a rebuild of both the bulwarks and the V-12 Deutz engine, a new raised deckhouse, arborite paneling with oak trim throughout the inside, and relocation to the aft deck of the hydraulic crane (a device that has so far been used to salvage two aircraft, both Cessna 185s owned by Wilderness Airlines, that sank accidentally while at dock). The upgrade increased the value of the *Nitinat Chief* to $450,000 and left only two things untouched — the tug's fir hull and its rugged reputation. "It's never been sunk," Widsten boasts. "That's commendable for a working boat of its age."

The *Nitinat Chief* could have done much worse than fall into Widsten's hands. This is a man with a history, too; his family roots date back a century on the British Columbia coast, to the founding of one of its earliest European settlements. Widsten's great-grandfather, John, was in the first wave of Norwegian immigrants who abandoned Minnesota for the more familiar-looking fjords of central British Columbia in the 1890s and founded the farming community of Hagensborg, twenty kilometres up the Bella Coola Valley from the

Pacific. For those would-be farmers, the task of clearing the forest to plant their crops proved daunting, occasionally even fatal. John died when he felled a tree on himself in 1922, leaving his eldest son to raise the family and chase the dream of success. Remarks Widsten, "My grandfather was sixteen — the eldest boy, and twelve kids in the family. He ended up with the responsibility of raising them."

The tall, willowy Widsten does not speak Norwegian, and his knowledge of family history has more holes than a log homestead. But he still exhibits the earnestness and work ethic of his forebears, including his father, Craig, the owner of a thriving fishing resort at Shearwater on nearby Denny Island. In that sense, Widsten and the *Nitinat Chief* make a good team. Both are quick to tackle a business proposition. Over the past decade, Widsten has tried a stint at the venerable job of handlogging — a term used to describe the independent logging of small, remote strips of waterfront forest. Handlogging began as work for seasonally unemployed fishermen, a process of finding a site and submitting a logging application to the provincial forests ministry. But handloggers would too often high-grade the timber, taking just the biggest and most profitable logs and leaving genetic rejects to repopulate the site.

Nowadays handloggers must compete in a closed-tender bidding system and are required to follow a strict silviculture plan for each site, typically 1.5 kilometres wide by 100 metres deep. Forests ministry officials claim they had no choice, that handlogging had become more professional, full time, large scale. Moreover, high-grading took a high environmental toll, making the Douglas fir virtually an endangered species on easily accessible sites on the central coast. Bringing handloggers into the twenty-first century was not easy, as attested by angry protests outside the ministry's Bella Coola Valley regional office. "They've taken the freedom away from the handloggers," Widsten laments.

In his quest to earn a living from the forest, Widsten even got his feet wet as a beachcomber, one of those nautical vagabonds who scrounges logs here and there as they escape the big logging-company booms or wash into the ocean through erosion. "Whatever I found was mine," Widsten recalls, noting that the forests ministry collected a nominal stumpage fee of fifty cents per cubic metre. "Without a doubt, it was the most fun work I've ever done." Beachcombers develop a sixth sense about their environment. In heavy rains they will migrate to areas prone to slides; if they find a log with a company stamp they will trace it back to the source as effectively as following a trail of blood. "You can cream it, follow it back as far as the wood goes." The richest piece of timber Widsten ever skimmed off the coast was a Sitka spruce worth $2,500.

That isn't the only logging Widsten has done. Only two years ago he logged 8,000 cubic metres from sixty-six acres on his Hagensborg property that had first been logged more than fifty years ago. Where environmentalists mourn the loss of biodiversity when old-growth stands are replaced by second growth, Widsten sees only a thick, satisfying crop. "It was outstanding second-growth quality. Beautiful timber. I don't see any ecological loss." Still, logging doesn't match the romance of beachcombing. Years after he gave up beachcombing because of stiff competition, Widsten remains infected by the lifestyle. An orphan log drifting in the currents can still excite him. "I evaluate each one I pass. I'll cruise down a channel, see a log and say, 'That's worth fifty bucks.'"

The *Nitinat Chief* eventually found steady work on the central coast hauling logging equipment for Fletcher Challenge, a New Zealand-based forest company. But business soon dried up: another logging giant, Interfor, took over Fletcher's timber holdings and put its own barge into service in the early 1990s. Since then, Widsten has operated a charter business, hauling forest executives, engineers, and tree-planting crews, threading his way through the labyrinth of channels on the central coast and charging a flat $1,100 a day, which includes three square meals.

It would be easy to say that between them, Widsten and the *Nitinat Chief* have pretty much seen it all when it comes to coastal logging. But today's assignment is a new twist for both of them, a run to King Island, site of an illegal blockade against old-growth logging by Interfor and its contractor, Kwatna Timber. A group of Nuxalk natives from Bella Coola and determined young environmentalists from around the globe have assembled at Fogg Creek to block logging and raise awareness of the destruction of North America's last old-growth temperate rainforests. The blockade has dragged on for almost three weeks during a prime period for timber harvesting. The idled loggers are not amused. The arrival of the RCMP arrest team is imminent.

Under ordinary circumstances it is only half a day's journey from Bella Coola to Fogg Creek. But there is nothing ordinary about this trip, an assignment that just might be sticking in the craw of the *Nitinat Chief.* Less than an hour after we depart, the tug's water pump breaks, leaving us drifting aimlessly. Widsten wades into the grimy engine compartment and successfully jury-rigs the water-fed cooling system so that we can inch along at six knots — about half the regular cruising speed. A new part is ordered by marine phone; it should arrive with a helicopter pilot tomorrow at Fogg Creek, a favor from a friend. "Bad news," Widsten confirms, dripping with sweat. "First time I've had a breakdown like this." No one complains. No one's in a rush. After more than half a century of backbreaking work, who could begrudge the *Nitinat Chief* an occasional visit to the chiropractor?

Our S-shaped route is as historic as it is visually stunning: west through North Bentinck Arm to its confluence with Burke Channel, then north up Labouchere Channel and west again through Dean

Channel to Fogg Creek on the northeast side of seventy-five-kilome-
tre-long King Island. Almost two centuries ago, Alexander Mackenzie
of the North West Company canoed this same route to complete his
"long, painful and perilous" journey across Canada in 1793, twelve
years before Lewis and Clark reached the mouth of the Columbia
River. Today this roadless, unmarked wilderness remains as mysterious as ever to British Columbians. It is still remote and inaccessible,
except for a brief period each summer when British Columbia Ferries
provides service between Bella Coola and Port Hardy, on northern
Vancouver Island. The service began in 1995, officially ending Bella
Coola's unique reputation as the place at the end of the longest dead-
end road in the province.

That road, Highway 20, is a rollicking six-hour drive that begins
in the Interior mill-and-cattle town of Williams Lake, heads west
through rolling semi-arid Chilcotin rangeland, and threads its way
down into the glaciated Coast Mountains before kissing the salty,
slate-green lip of the Pacific. Over the last hour or so drivers must
navigate a steep road simply known as The Hill, a long and frightening set of gravel switchbacks leading from the Chilcotin Plateau down
into the rainforests of the Bella Coola Valley. Conquering The Hill
has become a matter of motoring pride, and the bragging rights are
determined by the size and unwieldiness of the motor home.

For obvious reasons, most British Columbians have never been to
Bella Coola; they would have trouble even finding it on the map.
King Island might as well be on another planet. Almost no one has
heard of it. By rights, that should pose a problem for environmental
organizations such as Greenpeace, whose political clout is inextricably
linked to mainstream publicity. King Island looms as a logistical
nightmare, far from the eyes of the news media in a place the public
may care nothing about. But Greenpeace's battle to save the whales
was not fought in Vancouver's English Bay or Seattle's Elliott Bay but

on the high seas. And such is the case with the province's last vestiges of old-growth forest, now threatened by the unquenchable hunger of clearcutting. With 60 percent of the more than five million acres of forest in the mid-coast timber supply area older than 200 years — western hemlock, western red cedar, yellow cedar, and balsam fir — it is inevitable that both industry and its eco-opponents would be drawn here in battle.

By the looks of it, the moody West Coast weather is shaping up for a battle, too. Clouds drift like heavy smoke across the layered, hazy blue silhouettes of mountains rising to 5,000 feet, then spill down sheer granite slopes to fill up the valley bottoms. Squalls of rain fall in sharp vertical sheets down the channel. A bald eagle skims overhead without so much as a wingbeat, surfing the brisk afternoon winds. A harbor seal battens the hatches and exits straight down, as though tugged by some creature swimming below it. A small single-engine plane nervously navigates through the looming storm, a vulnerable wind-tossed swallow in a swirl of burning white ash.

On the far shoreline of North Bentinck Arm, two gillnet fish-boats are in the starting gate, hunkered into a couple of tight coves, awaiting the start of the Bella Coola River commercial chinook salmon fishery. It is a lucrative, much-anticipated run. Up ahead, where Burke Channel meets Labouchere Channel, a pod of killer whales gets a jump on the competition, working their way along the shoreline, their black dorsal fins knifing through the water surface. This pod of killer whales is one of sixteen pods that total 220 animals and range between mid-Vancouver Island and southeast Alaska. It feeds almost exclusively on chinook, switching in summer to the sockeye runs passing through Johnstone Strait on the east coast of Vancouver Island.

John Ford, research director for the Vancouver Aquarium, has shadowed the whales by boat, moving in after each feeding to sweep the water with a swimming pool net. He looks for fish scales — crumbs, you might say — to find out what the whales have been eating. Chinook turned up consistently in 100 samples analyzed at the federal Pacific Biological Station in Nanaimo. As Ford figures it, the chinook is a logical target: it lives year-round on the coastline rather than migrating far out to sea, and, as the largest Pacific salmon species, it gives the whales a bigger bang for the buck than, for example, a smaller pink. "They use the coastline as a barrier to chase them, corral them, and capture them. If you're going to chase a salmon, you're better to chase a twenty-kilogram salmon than a two-kilogram salmon." Fortunately, the chinook runs to the Bella Coola River have not yet been decimated by overfishing and habitat destruction, as so many other coastal populations have. In 1996 about 25,000 chinook spawned in the Atnarko River, the key tributary to the Bella Coola, which compares favorably with 21,300 in 1986 and 13,000 in 1976.

The central coast is also inhabited by a distinct population of "transients," estimated at 250 killer whales, ranging from southern California to southeast Alaska in groups of three to six individuals. Oddly, these transients feed exclusively on warm-blooded prey — harbor seals, Steller and California sea lions, dolphins, porpoises, sea ducks, even the odd moose, deer, and bear caught swimming from island to island. But not so much as a single salmon hits their belly. "They don't touch fish," Ford confirms. "It's incredible — without precedent, really, in a wild species of any mammals — such disparate lifestyles." A few days ago these transient killer whales followed a group of Pacific white-sided dolphins into the narrow entrance to Codville Lagoon on King Island, sealed off the exit, and ripped at least one to shreds as the rest frantically sought refuge on shore. A prawn fisherman who witnessed the incident provided Ford with a videotape documenting the whales' hunting technique. "It was incredible. They were doing this high-leaping strategy to either land on and kill them or to scare them to death. They were so close to the shore you wouldn't believe it."

As the *Nitinat Chief* continues through a maze of channels toward King Island, we pass the odd patch of clearcut, evidence that the rush to exploit the province's last old-growth forests has already begun. In fact, the process of razing the land is well advanced, proceeding at a pace that even the provincial forests ministry concedes is not sustainable. According to the current five-year plan for the mid-coast timber supply area, the current annual allowable cut of one million cubic metres must be reduced almost by half, to just over 550,000 cubic metres, to "prevent a major shortfall in the future timber supply." This is not the crazy rhetoric of a misguided environmentalist, but the conclusion of the ministry's own cautious forest planners.

But trees are votes in the fractious political landscape of British Columbia, and the relentless destruction of the forests continues. The fear is that the situation could even be worse than anyone knows. The ministry projections do not take into account several factors — including the loss of timber land due to the requirements of the 1995 Forest Practices Code and a provincial policy of preserving 12 percent of the land base as protected areas by 2000 — that could further reduce the forest land base and make current timber harvesting rates all the more dangerous. The code's requirements for protecting sensitive riparian zones around fragile fish-bearing streams alone have reduced the available harvesting area by an average of 5 percent elsewhere in the province.

And that's with a government stream classification system that's seriously out of whack. Just imagine if the ministry got it right. A 1997 report by the environmental watchdog Sierra Legal Defence Fund found widespread evidence of mistakes in the field, including the Port Alberni forest district, within which Nitinat Lake is located. Among the key findings: 40 percent of the streams in sixteen of eighteen cutblocks were incorrectly identified or classified; 82 percent of 101 streams examined were clearcut to both banks; only one stream was given the full twenty-metre management and fifty-metre reserve buffer stipulated by the code. The forests ministry conducted its own audit, and while it didn't agree with SLDF on every detail, it confirmed an embarrassing number of mistakes.

Blaming the problem, in part, on heavy workloads for ministry personnel and logging companies, SLDF's report stated: "A total of 19 stream reaches were either not identified on plans or not properly classified, six of which were confirmed fish stream reaches, and eight require further stream assessment to determine the presence of fish. Of the 63 stream reaches reviewed . . . 18 may not have received adequate protection." Asked to comment on the findings, Dan Powell, the ministry's operations manager for southern Vancouver Island, concluded, "There definitely were some streams that were misclassified and perhaps even missed. Certainly everything hasn't been going perfectly. They certainly had the potential of leading to damage to the environment."

Brad Widsten is quick to agree that too much timber is being cut too fast, that the province is putting short-term politics ahead of long-term sustainability. He's not about to hug a tree-hugger, but he figures the publicity generated through civil disobedience is actually a good way to focus attention on timber issues and perhaps come up with better solutions. He doesn't even mind that Greenpeace has imported a handful of protesters from Europe, one of British Columbia's key timber markets. But he is equally adamant that environmentalists are unrealistic, unaware, or deliberately ignoring the fact that logging is the economic lifeblood of small-town British Columbia, communities that grew up around the industry and now face collapse without it. "We all know it's going to change, but to come in and make wild accusations that it should stop is unrealistic. We can't all come here and live on welfare and simply walk around in the bush."

Loggers are quick to write off environmental protesters as a bunch of freeloading welfare bums who would like nothing more than to put working families out of business. It is clearly an inaccurate assumption. Environmentalists, especially those who devote their lives to the cause or are willing to risk arrest in acts of civil disobedience, are well educated, idealistic (but not without contradictions), and willing to make the personal economic sacrifices necessary to preserve the rainforest. Many will gladly live a simpler lifestyle free of the four-by-fours, snowmobiles, and other expensive, environmentally destructive toys that befoul timber towns. In representing the most ecologically barren landscape in the province — East Vancouver — ex-Premier Glen Clark went so far as to call environmentalists the "enemies of British Columbia." It is a ludicrous statement, typical of the pit-bull politics Clark has practiced during his term of office.

As for Widsten, the legal system's inability to deal swiftly with lawbreaking environmentalists grates on him. In cases of non-violent civil disobedience, provincial policy prohibits the RCMP from swooping in and making arrests. Logging companies first must obtain an injunction and enforcement order in the Supreme Court of British Columbia, a costly and cumbersome process that is made even more difficult in remote locales such as King Island. Amassing a police team for such an operation is a logistical and financial nightmare. Some fifty officers with special crowd-control training must be gathered from a variety of detachments around the central coast and Vancouver. Transportation, accommodation, and overtime costs must be considered, not to mention the arrest and processing of the violators themselves. Widsten contends, "If they break the law, they should be dealt with like you or me."

But the system works both ways. Fearful of protesters shutting down Interfor operations for a third time, logging supporters erected their own blockade in the Squamish River valley, a two-hour drive north of Vancouver. They ruled the valley as their private kingdom, allowing loggers through but keeping out anyone who refused to sign a petition stating that environmentalists should be made to pay for job losses in the forest industry. Worst of all, they operated with the tacit support of Premier Clark and Squamish mayor Corrine Lonsdale, two politicians who are only too quick to decry blockades erected by the "enemy."

As Widsten motors around the northeastern tip of King Island and up Dean Channel, west of Bella Coola, he points to a small outcrop of yarrow-covered granite on the north shore. It is Mackenzie's Rock. Or so we are led to believe. No one can really say for sure, but the rock is believed to be the point at which the explorer concluded his epic journey. Indeed, it would be a logical place to stop, offering a gravel beach pullout for canoes, a fresh creek pouring off the mountainside, a strategic view of the channel, and plenty of level room for camping. According to Mackenzie's journals, he stayed at the rock for several days, trading beads for salmon and seal meat, before wisely retreating to the Bella Coola Valley over concerns the natives would "shoot their arrows and hurl their spears at us." To mark his trip's farthest point, Mackenzie wrote on the rock in vermilion and grease: "Alexander Mackenzie, from Canada, by land, the twenty-second of July, one thousand seven hundred and ninety-three." To commemorate the historic site — now a provincial park — government officials in the 1920s sought to chisel these same words permanently into the rock. They blew it, flippantly inscribing "Alex" instead of the esteemed explorer's full Christian name, and misspelling his surname as "MacKenzie" with a capital K, thereby creating an enduring and embarrassing typo. A plaque erected next to the rock explains none of this to visitors. No wonder the Nuxalk of Bella Coola write the place off as "white man's graffiti."

By the time we arrive at rain-drenched King Island, just a short ride from Mackenzie's Rock, the *Nitinat Chief* is heralded with all the curiosity of first contact. Protesters nervously anticipating the arrival of police poke their soggy heads from beneath a patchwork of blue plastic tarps. A couple of young Nuxalks emit warrior yelps and run down to the shoreline for a closer look. And the *Starlet*, a humble, rust-stained, thirty-six-foot ex-fishing trawler, pulls into the only docking space available on Kwatna Timber's wharf in an attempt to block our access. The vessel is owned by the equally humble Forest Action Network, a group of two dozen activists founded two years earlier during the first illegal protests at King Island. With some pride, members compare themselves to Greenpeace twenty-five years ago.

At King Island, Greenpeace is represented by the venerable *Moby Dick*, a seventy-two-foot-long converted North Sea fishing boat. Painted green and white with a rainbow on the bow, the *Moby Dick* sits anchored just off shore, a motorized inflatable Zodiac — the pesky trademark of the environmental group — suspended from its port side. Within minutes Greenpeace's Vancouver-based forest campaigner, Tamara Stark, is on the marine radio, trying to contact us, curious about our identity. It is already dusk. We do not answer. Better to maintain journalistic silence until tomorrow morning in hopes of seeing the camp as it is, not as they would have it appear.

The early days of Greenpeace environmentalism — Zodiacs clashing with the high-seas whaling fleet, deftly dodging the bows of moving ships with dolphin agility — were laced with excitement, bravado, and at least the impression of spontaneity. In comparison, today's protests are as predictable as a Greek tragedy, as orchestrated as Beethoven's Fifth. King Island is no different. As we turn down the lights and call it an evening, we realize we have become — like it or not — actors in this unfolding play.

A small faction of Nuxalks is symbolically playing the lead role in direct opposition to the elected leadership of the 1,000-member band back on the reserve in Bella Coola. The rebels' spiritual head is hereditary chief Ed Moody, whose aboriginal name is Quatsinas, Spirit of the Raven. I find him the next morning, eating breakfast under the diffused light of a tarp, surrounded by the timeless smell of salmon and campfire smoke. Moody sizes me up with piercing, almost hypnotic, eyes — the perfect attribute to lead an army of idealistic eco-warriors. As Moody tells it — slowly, quietly, and methodically, a style of communication that has served the aboriginal system of oral history well over the past 10,000 years — the Nuxalk must fight now, before the big forest companies make off with the last of their traditional lands. "We want to protect the land and find a better way to manage the forests. In ten years it will be too late." One is reminded of the words of another practitioner of non-violent civil disobedience, Martin Luther King, Jr.: "The only real revolutionary is a man who has nothing to lose."

Moody has invited the participation of outside environmentalists: Greenpeace and Forest Action Network; Bear Watch, a group mainly dedicated to stopping the hunting of black and grizzly bears in the province; and People's Action for Threatened Habitat, a new group formed to fight logging in the upper Squamish and Lillooet river valleys, closer to Vancouver. In the fight not just to end clearcutting but to return control of traditional lands to aboriginal people, environmentalists are playing a vital role in the defence of these traditional lands, known to the Nuxalk as Ista. "They have the resources, the technical skills, and the techniques of how to use the system," Moody concedes. "It's a great way to get out the message. This is a global, international issue. We have common goals."

Moody's Nuxalk opponents in Bella Coola tell a different story. They claim the logging protest is a smokescreen set up by Moody to

delay coming to terms with his legacy of financial mismanagement —
more than $1 million in debt rung up during the four years he served
as elected chief before his defeat in 1995. Two years later he could not
even get elected to the lesser position of band councillor, and now he's
out on the front lines claiming to represent his people's interests and
inviting environmentalists from Germany and England and Belgium
to fly the Nuxalk flag. To Ivan Tallio, administrator for the Oweekeno-
Kitasoo-Nuxalk Tribal Council in Bella Coola, the protest is causing
more disruption in the native community than in the forest industry.
"The family part is the hardest. You'd like to talk to them but because
of the politics, you can't. It's not healthy for a community to allow this
to go on."

Since the blockade began almost three weeks ago, Interfor's logging contractor, Kwatna Timber, has taken the work disruption surprisingly well. Most of the thirty-five loggers have gone home, mostly to Victoria and Vancouver, which only highlights another gripe of
the Nuxalk protesters — outsiders taking forest jobs that belong in
the local community.

Only a handful of workers remain, including maintenance super-
visor Rob Mazurenko, who is based at a logging camp at Jenny Inlet,
just west of here. He visits each morning to go through the motions
and be turned away by the protesters. "We're a pretty tight bunch," he
says of his crew, a lump in his throat. "We see more of them than of
our own families." The logging company's only full-time, on-site
presence is caretaker Gus Gustafson. He sits outside his travel trailer
all day, every day, quietly monitoring more than $5 million worth of
idled logging trucks, pickups, trailers, and heavy-duty equipment.
Gustafson has spent the last forty years in logging on the British
Columbia mainland, Vancouver Island, and the Queen Charlotte
Islands and insists much has changed for the better in the industry.
But he is in no mood to change the world. "I'm not against anyone,"

he reflects, sipping coffee. "Everybody to his own thing."

Kwatna crews had logged up to 20,000 cubic metres of old-growth cedar, hemlock, balsam, and spruce before the protesters set up camp. The shutdown wasn't a complete surprise, and the loggers have been given instructions not to become embroiled in any physical altercations. To their credit, they have behaved admirably. In British Columbia's war of the woods, it hasn't always been so. Lord knows, it cannot be easy to sit quietly by while young foreigners try to eliminate your job and work to suck the self-esteem out of a once-proud profession. But it is still no excuse for the goon tactics loggers employed during an illegal logging road blockade set up by People's Action for Threatened Habitat in March 1997 at Interfor's tree farm in the Squamish Valley. Loggers slashed tires and dented vehicles. They physically jostled with protesters and splashed frigid river water over them. One logger even laughed while he feigned tossing gasoline onto the environmentalists as they sat next to a campfire on a gravel road.

If King Island is a measure of changing attitudes in society, the police are right off the scale, conducting operations with a combination of military precision and quintessential Canadian niceness. Sergeant Mel Petersen of the Bella Bella RCMP detachment leads an advance party aboard the sixty-foot catamaran *Inkster*, a new $1.5 million patrol vessel based out of Prince Rupert. He calmly navigates through the protesters' tangle of boats and makeshift squatter encampments, exchanging cookies for salmon and even telling the protesters the day on which the police team will arrive to end the protest siege. For Greenpeace members familiar with the harsh tactics employed by police and military commando units to end a range of direct-action protests around the world — protests aimed at nuclear weapons testing, toxic waste, whaling — the RCMP attitude is a pleasant surprise. "The police are quite nice," confirms Paul Ruzycki, an Ontarian who works four months a year as mate on the *Moby Dick*. "That's not always the case."

To appreciate just how much authorities have evolved, especially on the issue of aboriginal policing in this region, one must turn back the pages of history to 1877 and cast one's imagination just a little farther up Dean Channel to the old Indian settlement of Kimsquit. Believing that Kimsquit natives were responsible for the murder of the crew of the coastal steamer *George S. Wright*, authorities dispatched the Royal Navy ship HMS *Rocket* to make several arrests and shell the village to pieces. Seven long years later, in 1884, the village was compensated with $1,200 worth of lumber and building materials for new shelter, a requisition that came too late for those villagers who died of exposure after being left out in the winter's cold.

As the time of arrests nears at King Island, reporters drawn by the scent of confrontation begin to descend on the encampment. Some arrive aboard chartered float planes, others aboard $2,000-a-day pleasure craft from as far away as Denny Island. Sure, reporters are eager to exploit an opportunity, but they also serve a key role in the conservation food chain. Without publicity, would anything be spared? Environmental organizations could hardly survive without them. It is worth remembering that 90 percent of the province's $16.5-billion-a-year forest industry is export-based. If logging were to serve only British Columbia's needs, including those of its home-grown newspapers and environmental groups, and not, for example, the Los Angeles Yellow Pages, it would hardly make a scratch on the wilderness landscape.

As night falls, the police huddle over last-minute tactics and the protesters exchange anxious hugs. The reporters mooch for halibut, sip beer and wine, and, in a surreal touch given the circumstances, perform last-minute checks on their satellite-transmission phones and computers.

Early the next morning the RCMP arrive as expected: fifty officers trained in crowd control begin the task of making arrests, reopening the logging camp, and transporting the suspects to Vancouver for trial. Just twenty-four protesters — less than half of those who showed up — are willing to be arrested, including six foreigners and five Nuxalk clothed in traditional button blankets, chanting to the beat of a deerskin drum. Some are arrested on the main logging road beneath a banner reading "Standing Together to Protect the Great Bear Rainforest," championing the campaign to preserve the old-growth forests of the central coast. Some protesters are perched precariously atop a forty-foot-high wooden tripod. Others are affixed with bicycle locks to the fifty-foot-high steel tower of a grapple yarder. One man has gone so far as to attach his arm to a steel pipe buried in the logging road.

Seven hours later the show is over. The news reporters have their story, the protesters have their publicity, at home and abroad, and the loggers have their jobs back. And taxpayers foot the bill — a police tab of $68,000, two-thirds of that in overtime bills. One can only guess what the *Nitinat Chief*, the coast's elder statesman, might have to say about it all. It remains duty bound, tied to a boom log and taking in events with an owl's quiet wisdom — one eye on the logging industry's proud but profligate past, the other on its challenging, fractious future.

Perhaps Ed Moody spoke for more than himself moments before he was led away in handcuffs, a police dog snarling at his heels and a pod of killer whales cruising by in salute just offshore. "If I look at a book of 150 chapters, this is only the fifth," the Nuxalk martyr concluded. "We have a long way to go."

CHAPTER 6

# The Land of
# Bleeding Giants

*California's Redwoods*

WHEN GEOLOGIST Greg Gibbs parks his government-issue, four-wheel-drive vehicle and opens the security gate to the dark interior of Redwood National Park, there is a sense that he is unlocking a secret best left alone, a feeling that he is about to expose an unsettling truth about a magnificent natural icon. What better description for the redwood rainforests of northwestern California, home to the world's tallest living things, whose very existence transforms human delusions of superiority into quiet reverence and humility? That is certainly what occurs to the more than half a million visitors who each year travel the forty-five-mile stretch of coastal highway that links the 110,000 acres of four state and national parks — Jedediah Smith, Del Norte, Prairie Creek, and Redwood. To these pilgrims, the redwood forests are primeval last stands, ancient mist-enshrouded forests that

97

offer a rare glimpse of our prehistoric past and, yes, inspiration for our future.

Gibbs cannot entirely share their image. He has seen the god and it is false, an ecosystem whose fragility defies its apparent might, a place that tragically puts the lie to the adage "Time heals all wounds." The young federal geologist closes the steel gate, leaving behind the line of asphalt and convoys of waddling recreational vehicles on this wet September morning. He drives deep into the interior of the national park, to a place where a small army continues to do battle to save this precious landscape before it literally washes away into the ocean.

The environmental fight for these forests began in earnest in 1978, when the United States government expanded Redwood National Park by 48,000 acres at an eventual cost of $1.4 billion through a series of private land purchases. Considered a vital investment in the long-term ecological health of the region, these new lands were anything but pristine. Three-quarters of them had been logged since the 1940s, and all fell within the lower one-third of Redwood Creek — a watershed that drains 280 square miles on its 55-mile journey to the Pacific Ocean. Recognized as a United Nations World Heritage Site, the highest honor the world can bestow on a work of nature, the redwoods are certainly worth fighting for. But a combination of poor logging practices, naturally steep and unstable slopes, and heavy rainfall — most of it between October and May, the forest subsisting on ocean fog all summer — make for a formidable struggle.

California's northern redwoods are one of the most intensively researched rainforests in America's national park system. Scientists have studied the way in which the forest responds to wildfires and know how redwoods are able to reproduce by sprouting new shoots from their trunks or roots. They have observed the effect and frequency of gaps in the old-growth canopy, the rate of leaf decomposition on the forest floor, and the way bats make use of hollows in old trunks. And they remain fascinated by the forest's amazing biodiversity, from ground-dwelling fungi to a host of canopy-dwelling insects. But no aspect of the redwoods has been more intensively explored than the impact of logging, an activity whose effects become apparent after every violent rainstorm.

One such disastrous event occurred in 1997, when winter rains twice their normal levels flooded all the region's rivers, closing Highway 101 at Prairie Creek and cutting off vehicle access to Crescent City in the north. The storm caused more than $10 million damage to roads and infrastructure and closed several trails in the parks, including the trail to the famous Tall Trees Grove. A damage survey estimated that park logging roads alone were responsible for sloughing off enough sediment and debris to fill 25,000 dump trucks. It was dramatic evidence of what scientists throughout the temperate rainforests are discovering — that logging roads can pose a far greater environmental hazard than clearcuts.

Logging and the landslides associated with it strike a fatal blow to fish stocks, silting up and scouring spawning channels, stripping away creekside vegetation, and raising water temperatures to dangerous levels while eliminating the rearing and holding pools and the woody debris the fish require for cover. The cumulative effect is ecologically crushing. A century ago the Yurok aboriginal people maintained a seasonal camp near the mouth of Redwood Creek, where they fished for salmon, with spears in the shallow riffles and gillnets in the deeper pools farther upstream. Around 1920 a commercial fishery operated at the creek mouth, supplying the fish markets of nearby Eureka. A substantial sport fishery also grew as news of the area's productivity spread — coho salmon, cutthroat trout, steelhead, and, most impressive of all, chinook salmon the size of children.

By 1965, although fish stocks had declined significantly from historic levels, the California Department of Fish and Game still listed Redwood Creek as a major stream, with a spawning population estimated at 2,000 coho, 5,000 chinook, and 10,000 steelhead. Today, all species are gasping for breath on Redwood Creek. The runs of oolichan, an oily type of smelt the Yuroks dipnetted as the fish spawned in the lower reaches of the creek, are gone. The endangered tidewater goby, last caught in 1980 in Redwood Creek, may have joined them. And coho stocks are officially listed as threatened by the National Marine Fisheries Service.

The decline in fish stocks is blamed on natural flooding, sport and commercial overfishing, the construction of levees, and logging. But it is the latter that continues to pose the biggest impediment to rehabilitation. Summer steelhead runs, teetering on the brink of extinction with just a couple of dozen fish remaining, are especially vulnerable.

Adult steelhead swim up Redwood Creek in the spring, hold in deep pools over the summer, and spawn in the winter — a total of up to ten months in a watershed already exhibiting a weak pulse. Logging and siltation have raised water temperatures and plugged up many of the cool, deep pools required to sustain the steelhead through their freshwater cycle. Shallow water conditions and the sheer paucity of numbers also make the fish vulnerable to poaching.

The geology of Redwood Creek only compounds the problem. As the creek flows through the national park, it passes along a fault zone sandwiched between two distinct rock types, each causing its own problems. The east side of the creek is primarily underlaid with sandstone and is prone to gullying and earthflows; the steeper, wetter west side is a mica-quartz-feldspar schist, vulnerable to major landslides. Together they make for a landscape in constant turmoil, an ecosystem that has no opportunity to heal before the next onslaught of rain.

As Gibbs is discovering, it is as difficult to repair the wounds from logging as it is for a scab to form under a running faucet. Single-day downpours of three or four inches are not unusual in the watershed. Anything can — and does — happen on such days. Gibbs has observed scour marks almost ten yards up a tree, evidence of the volume of material that the mountains are capable of spewing downhill in a violent, rain-induced convulsion. "It's amazing," confirms the graduate of Humboldt State University in Arcata, one hour's drive south. "No one disputes that roads are the problem."

To begin the healing process, geologists in the park are busy removing the logging roads, pulling the culverts, and allowing the watercourses to return to their natural flow. Government workers have treated 200 miles of road at a cost of $13 million — that's anywhere from $10,000 to $250,000 per mile, depending on the gradient and instability of the slope. With almost 300 miles of unpaved logging haul roads and 3,000 miles of skid trails still needing rehabilitation, repairs have a long way to go. The exercise causes people like Gibbs to look askance at ideologically entrenched economists, foresters, and politicians in the Pacific Northwest who continue to assert the importance of logging to regional economies without portraying the other side of the ledger — the staggering environmental costs associated with repairing the damage.

Inside the park, near the headwaters of Tom McDonald Creek, a tributary to Redwood Creek, Gibbs pulls over at a road-construction site marked by three pickup trucks, a heavy-duty bulldozer, and a backhoe. Keeping well to the side of the road, we wade calf-deep through a wallow of rich, sticky, sweet-smelling soil that grabs at our boots. As Gibbs succinctly puts it, "It smells like life." Soon we reach the site of an active rehabilitation project supervised by Becca Smith, another frontline geologist employed to shore up the national park landscape. Dressed in a blue hardhat, yellow raingear, and orange safety vest, Smith explains that this particular road had been used for hauling logs since the mid-1950s. It typifies the second-rate logging practices of the era: when roadbuilding crews encountered the forty-foot-wide drainage channel on which Smith is now working, they didn't even bother to install a culvert, instead filling it up with an assortment of rocks, dirt, and stumps. Some stumps are still big and solid enough to be worth money in a market increasingly short of redwoods. Smith points to one fifteen-foot-high brute buried to its neck by loggers infilling the channel. "There was lots of wood when they were logging," she reflects. "Today, even that stump is worth a lot of money."

Logging on steep slopes can increase surface water flows to dangerous levels. Culverts are one way to reduce the potential for erosion through channeling, but at best they offer short-term protection against environmental damage. Old metal culverts erode from the bottom, allowing saturation of the underlying soils. Others are too small to handle the flows in raging storms. And others still, without maintenance — and sometimes despite it — plug up over time and spill over.

More than four decades after it was logged, this ravine looks benign enough, with no obvious flow. But Smith assures us that it would take only several days of persistent heavy rain to dangerously saturate the ground. With no culvert to collect the water and with much of the buried wood rotting and unstable, there is a real risk of it all sloughing off downhill and into the creek. Clearcutting can have a devastating effect on biodiversity, but when it comes to despoiling the land, Smith insists, "The roads are worse. They are what really damage the streams."

Work crews will keep removing all the introduced debris until they reach the old topsoil and reshape the ravine to its original form. When the crews leave, red alder will quickly exploit the lack of competition, swarm the streambanks, and help to stabilize the slopes. Because work like this effectively seals off portions of road from vehicle access, crews have to work backward in their goal of rehabilitating all logging roads in the park. It is a slow process, hampered by a short season for work crews; some sites cannot be entered until mid-September, to avoid possible disturbance to nesting marbled murrelets.

Gibbs returns to his vehicle and drives to another site. En route we pass through an active logging area owned by the industrial giant Louisiana Pacific and work our way into Bridge Creek, the site of some of the earliest rehabilitation work on national park lands and some of the steepest slopes in the Redwood drainages. Every so often the truck bounces over a water bar, a depression created after logging to siphon water off the gravel surface and prevent erosion to the roads. Gibbs stops at one section in which the shoulder of the highway has collapsed downhill in a massive slide — big chunks of gravel have been bitten off during the ravenous rains of winter. "This is a good one," he says sarcastically. "It gives you a sense of the water's power when it's moving." Looking down at murky Bridge Creek flowing in the distance, he adds, "Very close to where this slide entered the river, we found an additional three feet of material. My gut feeling is this is where it came from." There are no culverts at this section, and it is possible the slide started lower down and simply undercut portions of the roadway above. "Did the slide start here or stop here?" he asks. "The fact is, if the fill hadn't been put here, it wouldn't be in the river." As geologists are quick to discover, put a gravel bench on the side of a steep hill and nature's immediate instinct is to remove it, sweeping its skin clean of foreign substances. The process of healing is underway; a miniature forest of alder seedlings has already sprouted on site. But it is quite likely that the entire road will be washed downhill in the next big storm, long before the landscape has a chance to mend.

A short distance farther, Gibbs pulls over at Rodgers Creek, a tributary of Bridge Creek, and walks me through a dense forest of naturally regenerated alders that neatly camouflage a rehabilitation project finished in 1990. The trail is pockmarked with bear manure — evidence of the highest density of black bears in California. Struggling to pry away the alder brush, Gibbs says the invisibility of the road is evidence that the rehabilitation work is paying off. "If you didn't know what to look for, you wouldn't know it was a road."

From Rodgers Creek, Gibbs drives along a spur logging road, the M Line, leading northeast to Redwood Creek. He stops briefly at another yawning gap of hillside lost somewhere below and beyond. "This wasn't here before last winter," he says with the confidence of someone who spends up to three days a week in these forests. "You have to figure all that material went into Redwood Creek. The thinking is that it actually dammed the creek for a short period, then cut loose."

The Tall Trees Grove is just downstream from us, in the centre of the park, a ninety-minute drive from where we entered through the gate. Gibbs comments that the rains have arrived a month early this year, extinguishing hopes of an Indian summer and turning the logging road to quicksand. He decides to park the vehicle and walk the remaining fifteen minutes to the banks of Redwood Creek. Following a route lined with sword ferns as thick as cabbages, he informs me of the behind-the-scenes intergovernmental rivalry that exists in the redwoods. The state and federal governments may work together on management and research issues, but each wrestles for bragging rights to the biggest and best the redwoods have to offer. Redwood National Park, for instance, claims the tallest tree at 367 feet, a title subject to constant scrutiny and challenge. But Prairie Creek State Park claims the mightiest, a 1,500-year-old Goliath known as Big Tree, which by any standard is a tree and a half, measuring 313 feet high and 70 feet in circumference.

Normally Redwood Creek would be crawling with tourists from all over the world, but the closing of the main trail in last winter's storm has changed all that. Visitors must take the alternative route — a day hike over Dolason Trail that requires several creek crossings — and few are willing to bother given the rainy weather and brief period of daylight in fall. Besides, with so many monolithic trees to be hugged in the redwood forest, it is unnecessary to seek out this one — actually two redwoods, growing like burly Siamese twins from a common trunk. That the tall tree grows here is no accident. Redwoods flourish in the rich alluvial soils that dominate the lower flats of Redwood Creek, but they are also at greatest risk from a potentially dangerous cocktail of flooding, erosion, and an elevated water table.

Those who do make the pilgrimage to the Tall Trees Grove view only the lower extremities of these famous redwoods. From our vantage point, across the creek on the west bank, we can see a deformed head poking just above the crowd. "The one with the crooked top," Gibbs confirms. "That's the tallest tree." He adds that most tourists visit only briefly; they are reluctant to venture off the marked trail system. A short distance upstream, however, are some amazing but little-used gravel bars, perfect for camping and swimming in summer.

As the rain begins in earnest we walk back uphill to the Jeep for the long ride home. Along the way, Gibbs philosophizes about the way humans put themselves at the centre of events, then work back to find a solution. The redwood forests are a classic example. "We try to protect the land so it doesn't silt up the creeks so it doesn't kill the fish so we can have something to catch," he says. "We are here because we think we are making a difference. But in 2,000 years, what difference will we have made? The earth will be around long after we're gone."

He is correct in many ways. Survival of the fittest dictates that species come and go. Earth has already survived much more than humanity's excesses; the ice ages certainly transformed its face more than once. But it is equally true that we have lost much in a brief period of time. The old-growth redwood forests are no longer pristine or unsullied. They more closely resemble museum displays than fully functioning ecosystems. Several key species are missing — the wolf, the grizzly bear, the wolverine. Other types of animal life are in trouble — the marbled murrelet, the northern spotted owl, the bald eagle, the peregrine falcon.

Gibbs steers around a couple of black-tailed deer and a stone-stiff grouse sharing the logging road, then begins to navigate a final series of switchbacks corkscrewing downhill to the community of Orick, at the mouth of Redwood Creek. Suddenly he grinds to a halt. Our path is blocked by a heavy-duty truck pulling a bulldozer on a flatbed trailer, operated by one of the crews employed on the park rehabilitation project. The truck is trapped on a hairpin curve, the trailer jammed against a massive redwood stump that was left too close to the shoulder during construction of the logging road. The truck cannot go forward and cannot back up on the slippery surface without the risk of scissoring its way down an embankment.

As the trucking crew examines the possibilities, I seek refuge from the rain beneath a massive live redwood just across the road. It is one of those rare trees that miraculously escaped the chainsaw's bite before the area was declared a national park. Pressing my hands against its trunk, I note that the redwood is a unique species by any definition, but still begs comparison with other trees of the temperate rainforest. Its bark, for instance, is deeply furrowed and fire resistant like the Douglas fir, yet stringy and fibrous like the western red cedar. And its needles are flat and green, reminiscent of the Pacific yew.

Under the right conditions — a wet temperate climate within twenty miles of the Pacific coast — redwoods are prolific growers, capable of reaching forty feet or so in just twenty years and living for two thousand. The specimen before me, sporting limbs broader than the trunks of most tree species, existed long before the signing of the Magna Carta. The comparison is a fitting one. Just as all seems lost for the trucking crew, still scratching their heads and pacing back and forth in their steel-toed boots, a modern-day knight appears, wielding his sword. National park employee Don Frazier drives up in his pickup truck and pulls out the biggest, most frightening chainsaw I've ever seen — more than a yard long, perfect for cutting through the giant redwoods. Frazier nonchalantly sizes up the competition, fires up the saw, and tackles it as he would a brick of aged cheddar cheese, one wedge at a time.

This is a different war, and I am quick to appreciate how it used to take two loggers several days to fell the largest redwoods in the early 1900s. It takes Frazier ten minutes just to carve a single wedge, and three grown men, including me, to push it aside. Sweat spins off Frazier's forehead as fast as wood chips spew out of the chainsaw. Then the chain comes off. And the saw runs out of gas. But Frazier is undeterred; the stump must go. And so it does, in a manner of speaking. An hour later the log is bent but unbowed. Frazier has succeeded only in hacking off the corner closest to the road, just enough to allow the flatbed trailer to squeeze past. And no more. It is getting late; time for a truce. The redwood has made its point. It will probably continue to stubbornly govern this corner of the forest long after the rest of us are dead and gone.

Anxious for a souvenir of my experience in California's redwood forests, I am reluctant to resort to the garish fare offered in Orick, a hillbilly of a town. The streets are a hodgepodge of makeshift stands and curio shops filled with trinkets — grizzly bears, windmills, jewelry boxes, cigar-store Indians — all carved from the redwood logs that drift downstream in the winter storms. Not surprisingly, the town has the appearance of a place washed ashore at high tide.

No, I want a more personal memento. I reach deliberately into the heartwood of the redwood stump, pull out a small wedge of wood, and toss it into the back of Gibbs's vehicle. Because we are not technically in the park now, Gibbs does not have to look the other way or report me for illegally removing park flora. The wood is solid and strong, heavy with natural resins, sweet and aromatic in the humid forest. It is not from the tallest tree in the world, nor the biggest. But it is the stump that nearly stumped us all. In doing so, it renewed our respect for the living redwoods that remain.

CHAPTER 7

# Bear Country

*Fight at the Top*
*of the Food Chain*

GORDON GIROUX doesn't really want to shoot the bear. He is hoping for something bigger. Something he can mount and proudly hang on his wall. Something to fill his freezer with meat. Something that might make a good campfire yarn down the road. But Giroux is already halfway through his three-day hunting trip and has spent a bucketload of money. He's driven his borrowed beat-up pickup truck over hundreds of kilometres of logging roads, relentlessly scanning the clearcuts and gravel bars and sideroads for bears, and he can no longer afford to be choosy. Sure, it's a lazy man's hunt; Giroux is quick to admit it. But it's the reality in the thick forests of coastal British Columbia, where black bears melt into the brush as efficiently as shadows on a moonless night.

Besides, at fifty-three, Giroux has pretty much run out of options.

The Fraser River tugboat operator is overweight. He's already had one heart attack. And he suffers from emphysema and apnea, a disorder that causes him to stop breathing momentarily during sleep. But none of that prevents him from smoking two packs of cigarettes a day. "You only come this way once and I'm going to enjoy it," he insists, taking yet another deep drag. "Thank God for four-by-fours." His attitude toward "tree-huggers" and radical environmentalists is expressed in a T-shirt: "Earth First! Log the Other Planets Later."

Giroux stops on a wooden bridge next to the upper Pitt River Valley, a refuge of calm about an hour's journey northeast of Vancouver's two million residents. It is 10 a.m., and the spring sun is just beginning to inch its way into the deep, cool trench of the river valley. Giroux has always liked this spot for its wide sweeping views of the gravel bars. Some black stumps washed downriver and beached on the gravel may have fooled him before, filled him with false expectations, but not today. When he raises his seven-power binoculars to his eyes, he knows that the dark, stationary object 300 yards away is all black bear.

His first instinct is to defer to his hunting partner, Jack Drover, a forty-five-year-old former Newfoundlander employed in maintenance at the South Delta Recreation Centre in Vancouver's suburbs. But Drover's rifle, a .375 Winchester, is too small for the distance. Giroux's scoped bolt-action Browning is not. He loads the rifle with a Remington magnum cartridge, rests the weapon carefully on the hood of the truck for accuracy, and takes aim at the figure still standing behind a log. When he pulls the trigger, the quiet of the valley is shattered by a brief sonic boom as the bullet rockets out of the barrel at 850 metres per second, almost three times the speed of sound. At that moment, no act of man or nature can stop it. Even the wind seems to step aside and let it pass.

Giroux could have missed. Worse yet, he could have wounded the bear. But he's a good shot, and this time he gets lucky, too. The bullet smashes through the bear's ear, turns its brain to mush, and keeps on going out the other side. The bear crumples, just like that, dead before it hits the ground. "There is no rush or thrill in pulling the trigger and killing the animal," Giroux insists. "It's the sad part really, but it has to be done."

By the time the two men drag the kill across the gravel bar and dump it into the truck for skinning, it is no longer a bear, just a warm pile of flesh and skin, blood oozing from its nose, attracting a swarm of big black flies. No trophy here. The bear is barely three years old, measuring less than six feet even if it is generously stretched by a taxidermist. "It's not very big," agrees Giroux as Drover quickly strips the skin away from the hindquarters. "But what the hell, I needed some meat."

Rather than have it mounted at a cost of $700, Giroux will have the hide tanned for about $140 and use it as a throw. The meat will be cured or smoked and cut into ribs and chops. The gall bladder, prized as a traditional Asian medicine and worth $250 and up to the hunter on the illegal market, will be left to rot on the gravel bar along with the rest of the entrails.

Asked why he does it, why he has gone to so much bother to shoot that bear, Giroux says there is no single, easy answer. Part of it is his love of getting out into the wilderness. Part is the desire to shoot his own game rather than rely on the hormone-laced meat sold in supermarkets. And part is cultural. Although he now lives in suburban North Delta, Giroux got his first rifle at age eight, in rural southern Alberta. That was one year before he started smoking, and he isn't about to give up hunting either. But there is more to it. Something about the hunt, the act of finding game and taking it down in the wild, that brings him back year after year. "Sure, it's a blood sport," says the ex-president of the Burnaby Fish and Game Club, a longtime volunteer with the British Columbia Wildlife Federation. "No denying it."

Giroux admits he doesn't have to go bear hunting; he typically goes on five other hunts each year, for deer, moose, and elk. Each hunt costs $450 to $500 for gas, fuel, groceries, cartridges, and hunting fees. The rife is another $1,300. But the spring bear hunt traditionally is the start of the season. For the avid hunters it's a long wait until the other big-game animals come open in the fall. Besides, he argues, black bears are plentiful in the province and there is no conservation reason for not allowing people to hunt them. "It's not necessary," he confirms. "But I enjoy it."

Drover has hunted since his childhood in Newfoundland. His family could not afford store-bought meat and subsisted throughout the winter on moose and caribou. "It's part of me," says the resident of suburban Surrey. "I grew up with it, and you get comfortable with it." Drover has been to slaughterhouses and witnessed first hand the horror of the domesticated food chain — animals filled with terror moments before their death or still conscious when their throats are slit open on the assembly line. That, he says, is cruel, and anyone who supports such practices by buying meat in neatly wrapped packages at the supermarket should not point a finger at hunters. "I could take a gun and snuff out any living animal on this planet, but you couldn't pay me to work in one of those slaughterhouses."

There is one animal he has not snuffed: the black bear. Now it's his turn. On the road again, Giroux drives north up the valley for another twenty minutes or so, until the road pulls gently upward onto a bench. When he stops to look at a black-tailed deer frozen in the forest shadows, his attention is suddenly drawn to a movement nearby. "There's a bear! See him?"

Drover readies his rifle, steps out, and takes a look for himself. "Two of them," he adds, adrenaline swelling. Then everyone relaxes. "A mother and two cubs," Giroux concludes from the obscure tangle of moving fur. "We'll leave them alone." Under British Columbia's Wildlife Act, it is illegal to shoot a black bear in the company of cubs aged two years or younger.

Giroux continues on, taking a spur logging road high into Boise Creek, where waterfalls heavy with snowmelt hemorrhage from the mountainside. The higher we travel, the worse the road gets until we are bounding heavily over boulders and skidding through snow toward the cliff edge. "The little fat boy from Newfoundland is having fun," shouts Drover, peering over the edge. "This is better than sex, but I wouldn't tell my wife that. She'd kill me."

Giroux is familiar with the territory. "This is the area where I saw thirteen bears," he recalls, binoculars scanning the terrain for just one more. "I shot one from just over there, 200, 250 yards away. It went down like a ton of bricks. And that bear hanging on my living-room wall, Jack? I took him right there."

When no bears show up, Giroux heads back downhill, nonchalantly negotiating the logging road before he stops in his tracks. A bear walks out from the slash and starts across the logging road directly in front of us. Slightly smaller than the one shot by Giroux, it stops in the middle of the road, turns, and briefly stares us down. Now is Drover's chance. He need only step out of the vehicle, load, aim, and fire. "You want him?" Giroux hastily asks. But Drover doesn't flinch. This specimen is just too small for a man's first bear.

"No," Drover replies. "He's too small. I don't want to take a baby. I'll wait. I want something substantial. I don't want to go home and have my children say I shot a baby bear."

—

Environmentalists in British Columbia consider bear hunting an outdated practice driven more by the egotistical desire for a trophy than the need for food. In an effort to have the practice banned, they have tried everything from gruesome ads on television depicting bloody skinned carcasses, to a massive but ultimately unsuccessful campaign to force a province-wide referendum on the issue (an effort doomed to failure not so much by lack of public support as by the unreasonably high standards set by the province's initiative and recall legislation — to force a referendum they need to collect the signatures of 10 percent of the registered voters in all seventy-five electoral ridings within a ninety-day period). A few representatives of the more radical eco-fringe have risked arrest and personal injury by physically intervening in guided trophy hunts catering to affluent foreigners on Vancouver Island, torching taxidermist shops and hunting cabins in the Kootenay region, and mailing out razor blades allegedly laced with rat poison to hunting guides around the province.

The spring bear hunt is among the most contentious. Conservationists claim it represents a double standard, since other big-game animals are hunted in the fall. And they view it as ethically irresponsible because young cubs whose mothers are accidentally shot in the spring have little chance of surviving. One Ontario government study that led to the banning of the spring black bear hunt in 1999 estimated that one-third of the 4,000 bears killed each spring are female and that about 270 cubs die annually of starvation or attack from other animals. In spring in British Columbia, bears are also concentrated in the valley bottoms and lower clearcuts because of snow at higher elevations. Where logging roads funnel through these valleys and timber cutting areas, hunting holds all the sport of backyard target practice. Hunters also often prefer bears in the spring because their pelts aren't scuffed and scratched, they have less fat, and they don't smell of fish, as they can when a bear feeds on spawning salmon in the fall.

The debate continues on whether a bear straight out of hibernation is too groggy for a fair hunt — if such a thing even exists. I have reached my own conclusion. Of the dozens of bears I have spotted during twenty years of wilderness travel, only one — a big black bear alongside Murray Creek, high above the Thompson River Valley — seemed to exist in a sort of carefree, careless stupor. The month was April, only days after the bear had emerged from its den. It lounged lazily on its back, exposed and vulnerable in the noon sun, massaging the warmth into its absorbent black fur. Watching from across a creek, I could have walked up and dispatched it with a handgun. It would have been that easy.

British Columbia's management of black bears has made it a target of the anti-hunting movement. The provincial population estimate of 120,000 to 160,000 black bears is pure pin-the-tail-on-the-donkey. In truth, the government does not even know how many die each year. The estimate of legal kills — 3,858 in 1998 — is guesswork, derived from the generosity of hunters who fill out a questionnaire and return it to the environment ministry. And regardless of how accurate that figure might be, it represents only a fraction of the total black bear deaths. With underfunded conservation officers stretched thin across the province — as few as two officers patrol some northern districts the size of Switzerland — the ministry has no clear handle on poaching, much less on roadkill or other human-induced deaths.

Perhaps strangest of all, as these same conservation officers wage a vigorous public relations campaign against the illegal trade in bear gall bladders for the Asian herbal medicine market, they are quietly responsible for a huge slaughter of bears. In 1998 alone they shot 1,619 black bears for posing a threat to human life or property. That's way up from the 991 black bears shot by conservation officers in 1996, a number equal to 71 percent of the total legal hunting kill in Washington state. Officers also shot 36 grizzlies, twice the entire grizzly population in northern Washington's North Cascades.

You'd think every black bear in British Columbia would be dead by now. But no, they continue to thrive, which can be about the worst thing possible for a conservation campaign. The black bear is indeed a prolific species that seems equally at home roaming the remotest patch of alpine meadow as attending backyard barbecues in posh West Vancouver subdivisions. It won't always be so. Eventually the government's laissez-faire attitude to black bear management will catch up with the species as human exploitation continues to chip away at the wilderness and British Columbia paints itself into the same ecological corner experienced by so much of North America.

And you can bet that few factors will lead the bear to the brink of disaster faster than easy, unfettered human access to the backcountry. At last count, Crown logging roads — half of them abandoned, the other half maintained by the forests ministry or by timber companies under permit — ran for 300,000 kilometres through the British Columbia landscape, more than twelve times the amount of paved provincial highway. Open equally to the general public for recreational use and the forest companies for timber extraction, Crown logging roads are a glaring example of logging's impact on wildlife. Long after the last clearcut has begun to green up and grow trees once again, these logging roads remain in use, providing unrestricted access to critical wildlife habitat for four-by-four yahoos and motorcyclists in summer and ear-shattering snowmobilers in winter. And while the provincial Wildlife Act provides stiff fines for poaching violations — up to $25,000 for illegally shooting a grizzly — it still does not go far enough to protect bears in areas where they are most vulnerable to being shot.

For the grizzly, which lacks the black bear's tolerance for humans, the situation is especially grim as it is forced into increasingly remote and marginal habitat. *Ursus arctos* is a species that evolved in the forests of Asia two million years ago and crossed the Bering land bridge into North America 50,000 years ago. About 100,000 grizzlies once roamed the western half of North America, from the barren arctic tundra south to the high plateaus of central Mexico. According to scientific ranking of species at risk, the grizzly bear is threatened, one step away from endangered, in America's lower forty-eight states, where fewer than a thousand live in isolated populations, mostly in Wyoming's Yellowstone National Park. In Canada, home to about 10,000 grizzlies, half of them in British Columbia, the species is listed as vulnerable. But there are several pockets where grizzlies are in imminent danger of being wiped out (as they have been on the Canadian prairies), including the Granby Valley, the Selkirk Mountains, and the North Cascades, all on British Columbia's southern border.

Barrie Gilbert knows better than anyone the potentially disastrous implications of human-bear interactions. As a young assistant professor specializing in bear behavior at Utah State University's department of fisheries and wildlife, Gilbert was putting in his first day's field work at Yellowstone National Park in 1977. Crossing a remote ridge at 8,800 feet, he surprised what he believed to be a bedded-down grizzly sow. Two decades later, his face scooped out like a bucket of ice cream and a patch over one eye, Gilbert relives the ensuing confrontation with gruesome clarity. "It was the worst of all possible worlds. First day on the job. She ran me down, tore my face off and pretty near killed me. I spent two months in the hospital, and just about died from infection. I had half my face replaced with skin tissue from my shoulder. My eye was torn out, both ears were torn off. My nose had to be wired back on. I was almost completely scalped."

Rather than become embittered by the ordeal, Gilbert shook off the curious looks from passersby, and even his own repulsion at his image, and embarked on a lifelong quest not to restrain the grizzly, but to save it. In the 1980s he studied human-bear interactions in Katmai National Park on the Alaska Peninsula, where the seasonal availability of salmon before denning draws an estimated 550 bears per 1,000 square kilometres — up to twenty times the density of landlocked Yellowstone. Gilbert's latest research took him to the fjords of British Columbia's central coast, where he travelled for six weeks by inflatable boat into the remote heart of Rivers Inlet and Smith Inlet, navigating an all-terrain vehicle over pitted logging roads and "hiking some of the damnedest bear trails you've seen in your life." After walking for ten kilometres on one logging road, he came across a half-ton pickup truck that had been barged up to Owikeno Lake and parked near a hunting platform next to a stretch of salmon-spawning stream on the Nekite River. "It's drive-in bear hunting, killing bears at basically the only place they can come to feed," he concluded. "Is that ethical?"

Talking with native people living in the Owikeno area, Gilbert heard stories of up to five grizzly carcasses plugging a single stream. "There is potential for devastating overhunting of the coastal populations. It's like potting bears as they come by at a garbage dump." Flying over the central coast for two hours with Lighthawk, an American organization of environmentally minded aviators, he noticed that virtually every watershed was varicose-veined with logging roads, putting all bears at risk from similar unethical hunting, not just at spawning streams, but in estuaries and intertidal zones where bears fearlessly walk the beaches in search of mussels and other marine life.

Gilbert is now working with the Raincoast Conservation Society, the lead group fighting for preservation of the Great Bear Rainforest, the campaign name for a wilderness encompassing 8.4 million acres, from the southeast Alaska border to the bedroom communities north of Greater Vancouver. As Gilbert sees it, the provincial government simply lacks the political and economic will to tackle the hunting lobby and the big forest companies on the issue of bear management. "Native people lived with these animals for 12,000 to 15,000 years and we've obliterated them in less than 200. If B.C. thinks it's going to do anything different, it has rocks in its head. Their wildlife protection is no better than that in any other place. Timber companies almost run the B.C. government. British Columbians will have to ask whether they're not just another banana republic under international corporations. It really doesn't have to be tropical mahogany or coffee, you know. It can also be trees."

For an explanation of the province's failure to take on the hunting lobby, look no further than Dionys de Leeuw, senior habitat-protection biologist with the British Columbia environment ministry. He became so disillusioned with his government's hunting policy that he published an independent study of the subject. De Leeuw just couldn't understand why the province continued to allow trophy hunting of grizzly bears — an activity undertaken by fewer than one-tenth of one percent of the population, but opposed, according to one poll, by 91 percent. His inescapable conclusion? There is a built-in bias in the ministry that extends not just to hunting regulations but to preferential funding. For example, up to 80 percent of the total effort of the fish and wildlife branch is devoted to species that are fished or hunted. And over the last ten years, 70 percent of the approximately 1,000 projects approved under the Habitat Conservation Fund, a program funded by a special surcharge on fishing, hunting, trapping, and guiding licenses, concerned the promotion of game species. The bias even spilled over into the provincial park system, which rather than serving as a biological refuge for wildlife and for the enjoyment of the 91 percent of British Columbians who engage in wildlife-viewing activities, allows widespread hunting in most of the larger wilderness parks.

De Leeuw even attacked the commonly held belief that hunting is an integral and instinctive part of human culture evolved over countless thousands of years. If that is so, he asked, why do the overwhelming majority of humans today not hunt, have no desire to do so? And why, among those who do hunt, is the desire expressed so selectively, mostly in the fall (with, I might add, a few cases of beer and the company of a few drinking buddies)? De Leeuw's gutsy report, researched on his own time over a year, made him a target for environment ministry staff and the hunting community. Ministry staff flooded him with interoffice e-mail, some of it supportive, much of it hateful, to the point of calling him an outright liar. The owner of one gun-and-tackle shop on Vancouver Island went so far as to publicly suggest an open season on de Leeuw. And the environment ministry slapped him with a gag order prohibiting interviews with reporters for three months — well beyond the shelf life for most news outlets, which, when it comes to the rainforest, are more interested in today's story, be it the protest, the layoff, the gloomy financial statement.

According to de Leeuw, the ministry declined to tell him what it thought of his report, but one senior official did suggest in a radio interview that the number of hunters within the wildlife branch is probably close to 50 percent. "That's still ten times greater than hunter densities within the province," de Leeuw told me in his first interview after the gag order was lifted. "It's a major conflict-of-interest issue." In 1999 de Leeuw's boss, Environment Minister Cathy McGregor, shortly before being dropped from cabinet, provided him with the first good news since his report, declaring a ban on spring grizzly hunting in a large area of the East Kootenay region near Alberta.

By far the province's best grizzly habitat, however, is the temperate coastal mountain zone, running from southeast Alaska almost to Washington state, an area that supports up to 3,300 of the animals. Here the grizzly thrives on a mosaic of lush habitats, topped off by the seasonal spawning salmon, a diet that allows coastal bears to grow to twice the size of their Interior cousins. But the timber industry also prefers the big lucrative stands of timber on the valley bottoms, putting it in direct competition with bears that are trying to access some of their most vital seasonal habitat requirements — the juicy tubers of skunk cabbage, the fresh green shoots of sedgegrass, avalanche chutes, the berries of devil's club and elderberry, the nutritious carcasses of spawning salmon.

Bears may benefit initially from the flush of new berries in a clearcut, but they may take advantage of only the edges of large cutblocks because they prefer to stay close to forest cover. And when herbicides are used shortly after logging to kill off the brush and berries that compete with the growth of commercial seedlings, it alters the natural regeneration process. By the time a managed stand of trees is fifteen to twenty-five years old, it is a biological desert, too thick and dark and uniform to support much of anything except a tree thinner.

Logging also disrupts denning, it hacks productive bear habitat up into fragments, it targets old-growth forests important to bears for cover and denning, and, in a bizarre if relatively recent phenomenon, it allows the introduction of domestic sheep to feed on clearcuts, turning forest lands into pasture and robbing the grizzly of forage. Not surprisingly, a 1995 grizzly conservation strategy report by the environment ministry concluded: "Nearly all grizzly bear ecosystems in B.C. are at risk under current land use activities."

As a research biologist for British Columbia's wildlife branch, Tony Hamilton has quietly studied the effects of modern industrial logging on grizzly habitat for fifteen years. I first met him in 1986 during a five-day trip to the Kimsquit Valley, north of Bella Coola on the central coast, site of a five-year study of logging and grizzlies. Like a mustachioed wild-west gunslinger, Hamilton carried a pump-action 12-gauge shotgun as he waded into a dense growth of devil's club beneath a stand of tall cottonwoods. "There are only two kinds of animals in the world," he jokingly told me. "Bears and bear food." The truth, however, is that the ravenous appetite of Doman Forest

Products Ltd.'s modern industrial logging took a huge bite out of grizzly activity in the area. When logging stopped one year for economic reasons, researchers sighted grizzlies sixty-seven times from the logging road, including forty-one times at a critical spawning area. When logging resumed the next year, there were just sixteen sightings — only two of them during active log hauling, and none at the spawning bed.

Since then, in his own level-headed and well-balanced way, Hamilton has continued to document the damaging effects of logging on bears, not just from road access but from the intensive harvesting of valley bottoms to meet industry's gluttonous appetite. With too many mills searching farther and higher for wood supply, the annual cut is simply not sustainable, he concludes. As a field biologist familiar with the notion of survival of the fittest, Hamilton awaits the day when a reduced number of mills starts dealing sanely with what remains. "To be totally blunt, I'm waiting for the day it's no longer economic for harvesting. It's sad. We hear the news of mills going down, 2,500 people out of work, but there's just too many mills out there. Out of frustration, I get to the point I just wish it was over with, that the mills had gone down, and we can start dealing with what's left. Maybe we'll get the habitat after that. I know that sounds cynical and pessimistic, but I honestly think it's time to start talking that way."

The window of opportunity for Hamilton's prophecy opened in 1997, when an economic downturn of the Asian markets ravaged British Columbia's export markets. But instead of viewing the downturn as a time to regroup, to refocus on sustainability and value-added industries, the government chose in 1999 to soften its policies on stumpage fees and the amount of wood that companies are allowed to leave behind in clearcuts. Worst of all, the province also opted for a record $325 million bailout — an amount ten times the annual parks budget — to prop up the antiquated, unprofitable Skeena Cellulose mill in Prince Rupert, located in the riding of a key cabinet minister.

Quick to exploit commercial timber in the temperate rainforest, the province has been much slower to capitalize on the eco-tourism potential of bear viewing despite Alaska's success at McNeil River, Brooks Falls in Katmai National Park, Fish Creek near Hyder, and Anan Creek by Wrangell Island. Part of the problem is that there are few classic spots to which grizzlies are attracted for an easy salmon meal; the other part is that the province knows even bear viewing has its problems. "I wouldn't want it promoted as a benign activity," Hamilton says. "Viewing can displace bears from preferred areas just as readily as industrial activity can."

Bears can also alter their behavior in response to the presence of humans. Researchers suspect that young bears and females with cubs use such viewing sites as protection, knowing that the big males are reluctant to come around when humans are present. On the flip side, when bears begin to see humans simply as innocuous loiterers on the landscape, they become more vulnerable to being shot when they step outside of protected areas.

The Khutzeymateen Valley in the Coast Mountains northeast of Prince Rupert became Canada's first grizzly reserve in 1994, a 443-square-kilometre expanse of glaciers, avalanche chutes, bogs, flood-plains, old-growth Sitka spruce and hemlock forests, and salmon-spawning streams. Visitors stand an excellent chance of seeing grizzlies in the Khutzeymateen, especially in spring, when the bears are feed-ing on sedgegrasses in the open estuary. Give the park's remoteness, however, it is really a destination for the affluent: five-day excursions from Prince Rupert cost $1,500.

Of course if you're the do-it-yourself type, there are few better places to try your luck than the Atnarko River, a glacier-fed tributary of the Bella Coola River, which meanders through Tweedsmuir Pro-vincial Park, one of North America's largest wilderness parks, before spilling into the Pacific Ocean at North Bentinck Arm. Each fall the Atnarko River turns blood red with up to 3.5 million spawning salmon — pink, chum, chinook, coho, sockeye, and steelhead — making the watershed the most productive on the central coast. Although the river system is known more for its angling opportunities, up to fifty grizzlies are also drawn to the valley from as far afield as 140 kilometres.

The same attributes drew Stefan Himmer to the rainforest. A private grizzly researcher, he is one of a handful of people lucky enough to reside within Tweedsmuir in a home built prior to the creation of the park in 1937. His place once belonged to Tommy Walker, the legendary guide-outfitter who sparked a successful campaign for preservation of not just Tweedsmuir but also Spatsizi Plateau Wilderness Park in northern British Columbia. The home is located on a small gravel terrace above the Atnarko River, within a grove of old-growth Douglas fir that offers a sweeping view of a cottonwood flood plain interlaced with rose bushes, high-bush cranberry, black twinberry, and Pacific crabapple. And for all of this grandeur — the property is officially 3.5 hectares, just over 8.6 acres, but blends seamlessly into the rainforest — Himmer pays rent of just $500 a month. "When I first moved in, I got it for $400," he explains. "Rent recently went up. But I'm not complaining."

There is no one hot spot for bear viewing on the Atnarko River, just an estimated 100 kilometres of spawning channels meandering through the park. Bears could turn up anywhere around here, including Himmer's backyard. Or the front of his business card, which depicts a newborn cub on its hind legs, scratching its back on a tree. It is an amazingly lucky photo, taken with a 35-millimetre auto-focus, auto-exposure camera linked to a 12-volt battery and infrared sensors. The gizmo was designed to detect bears taking advantage of the mark tree, which in this case is an old-growth western red cedar used for scratching or rubbing by bears passing through the area. Himmer is proud of this photo. "It's my best shot," he beams. "Most are flash. But this was natural light coming through the forest."

Himmer began studying grizzlies as a contract researcher in 1990 in the Khutzeymateen Valley. He moved to the Bella Coola Valley in 1992 to investigate grizzly-human interactions on the Atnarko. His most recent project is also his most ambitious — a $200,000 DNA study of grizzly populations in the Kingcome and Wakeman River valleys on the central coast. Using salmon bait next to strands of barbed wire designed to collect the hair of passing bears, Himmer and his crew collected 3,000 samples to be run through a DNA lab in Canmore, Alberta, in order to identify individual bears by sex and species. The idea is to take the guesswork out of estimating grizzly populations. Estimates so far have been ballpark at best, determined largely by aerial photos of habitat. With Wakeman and Kingcome sealed off by glaciers to the east and south and by the Pacific Ocean to the west, there is less risk of bears moving in and out of the valleys during the two-month study period. It's hoped the results will bring researchers closer to knowing absolute population numbers, the first step to better management of the grizzly and to accurately judging the impact of logging and hunting.

Himmer is not opposed to subsistence hunting, and he pops the occasional moose, deer, and caribou himself. But the concept of killing a grizzly bear for sport, with no interest in the meat, is a concept he cannot understand. "I'd like to see it end. I can't see why someone would do it." While loggers have become more sympathetic to the needs of wildlife over the last five years, he says, the forest industry still has far to go. Access provided by logging and the sheer scale of the clearcutting remain the biggest threats to grizzlies on the central coast. "I don't think you could ever say you could enhance grizzly bear habitat by logging."

Although there's been no grizzly attack on a human in Tweedsmuir for some twenty years, the two species maintain a wary coexistence. A few years ago, mushroom pickers were suspected of killing two grizzlies they encountered in the bush. To help ward off further problems, Himmer has recommended that park officials relocate one kilometre of Stillwater Trail, close other trails between dusk and dawn, impose tight restrictions on anglers handling bait and gutting fish, and relocate one provincial campsite away from spawning grounds. The measures are designed as much to protect people as the bears, Himmer agrees. "It becomes a safety issue when meeting a bear at close range. Bears lose their fear and become unpredictable."

Anxious to find a bear on my own, I drive eastward through the park to where Highway 20 rises steeply uphill to the Chilcotin Plateau, and divert onto a rough gravel road hugging the bank of the Atnarko River. Signs of bear are everywhere. A sign by the garbage dumpster reads: "You are in bear country." Another announces a hiking closure at Hunlen Falls and Turner Lake due to "high bear hazard." And yet another warns: "Wild animals, especially bears, are potentially dangerous. Keep well away."

Undeterred, I follow an old homestead trail that runs up the valley. The route is heavily rutted by the fall rains as it winds through stands of old-growth cedars and cathedral-like canopies of alder and cottonwood. The smell of salmon hangs heavy in the humid coastal air. Spawned-out carcasses lie among the boulders on the river bottom and are washed up on the shoreline, eyes plucked out by marauding gulls.

Parking my pickup behind a clump of trees, I await the approach of dusk with a quick dinner of nacho cheese chips and sardines. This sort of meal is not normally recommended for grizzly territory, but given the all-pervasive stench of fish it's about as risky as passing wind at a garbage dump.

Just below me, on the other side of a clump of boulders, is a flat rock offering a sweeping view of the river. For a while I sit silent and unmoving, the sense of anticipation sharpening my senses. Then a sudden shuffling, right behind me . . . and a cry of alarm. "Meep!" It's a pika, for God's sake — a creature somewhere between a mouse and rabbit on the evolutionary scale — mouth full of grass, staring me down. Wondering if the cheeky beggar has given me away, I return my gaze to the river and wait. A giant salmon erupts from the darkened waters and slaps the surface right in front of me. Can my heart take much more? Can the sight of a grizzly be any more unnerving? Methinks so. Across the river and just downstream a branch snaps with a loud thwack. No pika this time.

I strain to listen. But there is nothing. Not a sound, not a movement. Just growing darkness. It is getting too cold on the rock, so I scramble up the bank and ever so quietly pace back and forth on the road. Time passes excruciatingly slowly.

Then, just as I am about to give up and light my campfire, I hear a muffled sound coming from downstream. Checking over my left shoulder I see two pudgy grizzly cubs working their way up the bank and onto the road. Their mother follows, her chesterfield-sized frame silhouetted against the full harvest moon.

She stares in my direction, rises on her hind legs for a better view, then drops back to all fours. Suddenly she and the cubs are gone, fleeing from me, running down the same access road that brought me here. It is not the image we associate with grizzlies, especially a mother with cubs. But in a world where bears that become too familiar with humans wind up dead, it is the right thing to do.

# CHAPTER 8

# The Secret World of Mushrooms

*Oregon's Mushroom Mafia*

AS I WAIT anxiously inside the United States Customs office at the Pacific Highway border crossing, detained while an inspector and drug-sniffing springer spaniel work their way through the cab and rear canopy of my pickup truck, it occurs to me there are easier ways to investigate the strange yet integral relationship between mushrooms and the temperate rainforest. I am also profoundly aware that it is risky business to entrust one's freedom to such a genetically challenged breed as the springer. To wit: a history of progressive retinal atrophy; hip displasia; bloat; epilepsy; skin allergies; blood disorder manifested by dark urine, pale gums, fever, and poor appetite; and — I'm not making this up — "springer rage," in which the dog erupts in a fit of biting, only to return to normalcy moments later as though nothing had happened.

Perhaps I worry too much. I do not use drugs. I have no criminal record. I have never been arrested. I have nothing to hide. Well, perhaps. In truth, there is more than enough paraphernalia in the customized wooden compartments of my pickup bed to raise the suspicion of federal authorities: two boxes of fishing tackle, but no state fishing license; a pressurized can of bear pepper spray; and a gift from my brother Brian — an ornate knife with a very sharp blade emblazoned with the image of a grizzly bear. True, these are simply tools of the trade for a biographer of the wilderness. But they could just as easily be viewed as evidence of a soldier of fortune, providing all the circumstantial evidence necessary to send me packing back to Canada.

When the officer in the booth asked why my friend Tracey Innes and I were entering Washington, I told him we planned to visit friends on Whidbey Island, a two-hour drive away across a body of water named, as fate would have it, Deception Pass. I thought my answer was sufficient, reasonable, straightforward. But the officer took one disparaging look at the back of my truck and ordered me to park next to the customs building and walk inside for further questioning.

That's about the time I felt I should volunteer a fuller story about my trip, which, by definition, was an underground operation. I told this second officer I was headed south to pick up a delivery of mushrooms. Not the bland, domesticated variety found wilting on the supermarket shelves. And not the magic or hallucinogenic psilocybin mushroom either, a forbidden fruit and Canada's only temperate rainforest native, which, once picked, can result in arrest for unlawful possession under the Controlled Drug and Substances Act. No, I am seeking the cream of mushrooms — the truffle, a tasty little nugget that lives entirely underground and features none of the stems or showy caps normally associated with the family of fungi. More precisely, I am after the wild Oregon white truffle, which at US$10 an ounce plus shipping is dearer than a rock of street cocaine.

I am receiving the truffles from Portland supplier Daniel W. Wheeler, who maintains an Internet website that almost begs a response: "A SIMPLE GUARANTEE — No money down! Don't pay until you're satisfied! If not delighted with my truffles, return by Express Mail." But getting Wheeler's truffles proved more complicated than the offer. Two U.S. courier companies spurned the liability risk of shipping unrefrigerated food, knowing it might take several days to reach its Canadian destination. The U.S. Postal Service didn't seem a much better idea, since the parcel would almost certainly be detained by yet another dog — Canada Customs employs beagles to sniff out food items. Hence my current plan, to drive to Whidbey Island to meet Tracey's friends, who have agreed to accept the truffles and keep them refrigerated until our arrival. When I finished relating my story, the customs officer looked at me, smiled, and acted like he understood my plight. "Truffles. They're a delicacy, right?" And that is when he told me to stay put while he and the dog went outside to do their business.

Yes, it seems like a lot of time, energy, and money for me to invest just for a mushroom. But the fact is, the more I learn about the culture of the temperate rainforest, the more I want to immerse myself in its wonder. I had smelled it, breathed it, touched it. It was time to eat it. To that end I had enthusiastically acquired Nancy Turner's handbook, *Food Plants of Coastal First Peoples*. With this compendium of more than 200 native plants, I dreamed of living off the land on my frequent forays into the wilderness, unshackled by freeze-dried meals, variety porridge packs, and Del Monte pudding cups. Or so I thought. Aside from describing the seasonal abundance of wild berries, which I pretty much knew about already, the handbook contained some of the least-appetizing recipes in cookbook history, serving up one gut-wrenching suggestion after another: the hardened pitch of Sitka spruce, to be chewed like gum; boiled cow parsnip stems, not to be confused with the "violently poisonous" water hemlock; steamed sword fern, regarded as "starvation food only" by natives; and roasted skunk cabbage stalks, which "contain long, sharp crystals of calcium oxalate, which, if taken into the mouth, become embedded into the mucous membranes and provoke intense irritation and burning." Clearly I would have to look elsewhere for my Gaian communion, my symbolic spiritual oneness with Mother Earth, my draw-first-blood response to the thought of bugs and worms rendering my spent body into soil in the eternal blue-box of life. As one truffle expert wrote: "Today mushrooms feed me, tomorrow, I them."

But my quest for the wild mushroom — and the quirky truffle in particular — is born of more than culinary interest. In the underground world of fungi, of which the mushroom is simply the visible fruiting body, lies one of the great secrets of the rainforest. It is here that we find the symbiotic relationship between fungi and tree, the giving and taking of nutrients and root matter that allows each to thrive . . . and which, once broken by ignorant timber-cutting policies, can lead to mutual ruin. It is a relationship I plan to pursue, but for now I surmise the customs inspector already knows enough. After ten minutes he returns to the office, hands back my car keys, and announces I am free to go. He even smiles and offers a reason why his colleague may have detained me in the first place: "He may have thought, there's all these officers just sitting around inside. Let's give them something to do."

During my uneventful round-trip to Whidbey Island to pick up the goods, it seems ironic that I should have to go through such hoops at just the suggestion of picking up wild mushrooms. What awaits me on my return to Canada, when I actually have them in my possession? As it turns out, my worries are for naught. A reflection of the fact that American authorities are more interested in drugs and their Canadian counterparts more concerned with taxation, the customs officer simply asks how long we were in the U.S. and how much we spent, then waves us on without even inquiring as to what we actually purchased.

When I arrive home in the Canadian border town of Tsawwassen late that night, I am quick to open the cardboard packaging, unzip the top of the plastic baggie, and dive in nose first for a deep breath. I have been told that the Oregon white truffle emits an aroma similar to garlic or cheese . . . and I have been misled. Perhaps it is the plastic, but this stuff exudes pure evil, a debilitating scent that deserves no place in the human intestinal tract. Not surprisingly, the truffles, which resemble hard potato nuggets the size of big marbles, just sit in my fridge, growing spongier and less appetizing each day.

On the morning of the fourth day, however, I steel myself, plug my nose, and slice off one-third of a truffle. Choosing to cook it with something mild that won't mask the, ahem, aroma, I fry it up with two scrambled eggs, cheddar cheese, and a dash of black pepper. Then I carefully swallow a forkful . . . and am amazed at the result. That something so nasty smelling can taste so subtle once cooked, can complement the meal so effectively, is indeed perplexing. I take another bite, and another, until it is all gone. And that is about the time I notice something is wrong. My mind and body feel out of sorts, my arms tingle and feel like rubber, and the multi-colored cover of my Oxford dictionary glows with insightful neon splendor.

Having almost died ten years earlier from a single, inexplicable allergic reaction, that is my first and most immediate concern. I reach for my mycological bible — *Mushrooms Demystified*, by David Arora — and thumb to the relevant section. It reads: "Another common type of mushroom poisoning is imaginary — people who have lingering doubts about the safety of their meal are apt to experience discomfort whether or not there is a physiological basis for it." Could it be? Or is there a reason the truffle I put out for the squirrel that uses the nest box in my backyard remains uneaten?

After an hour the feelings subside, but the mystery remains. Determined to resolve it that evening in Hunter S. Thompson fashion, I
try a second meal of truffles and eggs, this time experiencing none of
the discomfort and all of the culinary pleasure. It is now time to go
beyond eating, to scratch beneath the surface and reveal the true inner
nature of the mushroom. To do that I must travel to Oregon and ac-
company Wheeler and his band of fungi aficionados as they quietly
forage for the hidden secrets of the rainforest.

—

The monthly meeting of the North American Truffling Society is
now in session. Seven men and one woman stand in the morning
drizzle on the shores of Lake Hebo, fastening their yellow and green
raingear, pulling on their black gum boots, and sizing up their wea-
ponry. Each of these nouveau hunter-gatherers carries a mace-like
rake with a long wooden handle ending in a four-pronged steel claw.
This might make a picture of intimidation in the dark, decaying
streets of urban North America, but it generates little more than
curiosity here in the humid understory of Siuslaw National Forest in
northwestern Oregon. As I wade into the group armed only with a
pen and notepad, I am greeted by their ringleader, Frank Evans, an
electronics engineer from the small and, not surprisingly, nut-grow-
ing community of Dundee, an hour's drive away. "It's an esoteric pursuit," he confirms. "Well-suited to eccentrics like me."

Founded in 1980, the Corvallis-based society claims to be the
largest of its kind outside Europe, with 300 members from as far
afield as New Zealand, Sweden, and Mexico. As the only founding
member still active in the society, Evans holds the distinction of truffle master, the person responsible for finding interesting and challenging locations for the handful of hardy enthusiasts who show up

on cool, overcast days like this. That would include Pat Rollinson, a retired science teacher who, following the grand European tradition of training domesticated dogs and pigs for truffling, once tried to teach her pet Yorkshire boar Bunky to roam the rainforest in search of truffles. "He used to ride up front in the International Scout," Rollinson warmly reminisces. "He would almost cause accidents when people saw him through the window."

When it came to truffles, however, Bunky was as anti-social as they come. He would gobble them down with typically piggish enthusiasm if you shoved some in front of him, but no amount of coercing could force him to sniff one out on his own. Through no fault of his own, it turns out. By releasing chemicals that mimic the pheromones of a boar, certain truffles act as a natural lure for sows, but do little to stimulate the hormones of males. "It was hopeless," Rollinson muses. "He was the wrong sex."

Aside from its quirky cachet, its glamorous image, and its underground existence, the truffle is much like other mushrooms when it comes to filling its niche in the temperate rainforest. In the same way that apples relate to trees, truffles and mushrooms are the fruiting body of the larger and more complex kingdom of fungi. And while the showy edible parts steal our attention on rainforest walks, it is the lowly fungi that handle the ecological workload, quietly toiling beneath the surface to create the magnificent web of life known as the temperate rainforest. It is that simple, and that complex.

Mycologists categorize the untold thousands of varieties of fungi into three general categories. The first is saprobic fungi, which essentially assume the important role of the rainforest vulture, breaking down leaves, stumps, logs, and other woody debris and converting them to soil. Second is pathogenic fungi, which kill off otherwise healthy trees and, in doing so, create snags and open up the canopy to sunlight to enhance biodiversity. And third, and perhaps most important of all, is mycorrhizal fungi, which are locked into a critical symbiotic embrace with the root system of the rainforest.

The body of these mycorrhizal fungi, which include truffles, is the mycelium, an intricate network of fine, hair-like strands that acts as a complex highway system allowing the transportation and interchange of life itself. Once attached to the roots of a tree, the mycelium reaches far into the soil to provide its partner with water and nutrients such as phosphorus and nitrogen that would otherwise be out of reach, and, in doing so, provides the tree with an extra measure of insurance against drought and pathogens. In return, the photosynthetic tree releases carbohydrates, including sugars and vitamins, that are essential to the fungi's survival.

So important is this relationship that certain mycorrhizal fungi are marketed for the inoculation of landscape shrubs, flowerbeds, trees and shrubs, even commercial forest plantations, to promote rapid root development. For high-production nurseries or seedling operations that cannot devote individual attention to their plants, the fungi provide an extra edge against potential health problems and allow the plants a better chance of making it through the transplant process. It is easy to understand why scientists describe fungi as the foundation of the rainforest, the building block upon which trees are created and each tree-dwelling species of wildlife is ultimately dependent. The truffle is a prime example of this interconnectedness, providing food for red-backed voles and northern flying squirrels, which spread the fungi's reproductive spores through the forest before being consumed by predators further up the food chain, including the endangered northern spotted owl.

That the public remains ignorant of the life-giving role played by fungi despite the efforts of hundreds of environmental groups in the Pacific Northwest dedicated to preserving the greater web of life is a reflection of its unglamorous, unmarketable subterranean nature. Appearing to be nothing more than a tangle of minute, hair-like fibres, mycelium is easily overlooked by the biodiversity hucksters in favor of dramatic, easily understood examples — the grizzly bear, the salmon, the old-growth tree. Selling mycelium, it would seem, is no easier than electing Bob Dole.

But here is the reality: while a walk through a typical patch of coastal old-growth forest may yield an amazing diversity of sizes and shapes of trees, the actual number of species remains fairly small, a handful of key conifers typified by Douglas fir, western red cedar, western hemlock, balsam fir, and Sitka spruce. What makes the rainforest so biologically rich are the lesser lights, the untold thousands of species of mosses, liverworts, lichen, insects, and fungi that have adapted to fill their own niches, from the upper canopy down to the soil.

It wasn't until President Bill Clinton's 1993 forest plan for the Pacific Northwest — an area of the United States extending west of the Cascade Mountains to the Pacific Ocean and north from San Francisco Bay to the Canadian border — that the diversity of the rainforest ecosystem finally got the political recognition it deserved. Under terms of the plan, scientists created an inventory of 409 life forms considered at risk within the old-growth forest habitat of the northern spotted owl. Fungi accounted for 234 species, or 57 percent of the total. Four out of every five of those were mycorrhizal fungi, with more than half of them deserving the highest form of management protection against the destructive effects of clearcut logging. So rare are they that one fungi, *Gastroboletus imbellus*, has been found only once, twenty years ago, at Lamb Butte Scenic Area in Oregon's Willamette National Forest.

—

To learn more about the ecological precariousness of the fungi, I ventured to Corvallis, home of the "Mushroom Mafia," the seventy to eighty fungi researchers associated either with government agencies or the campus of Oregon State University. There I went foraging for Michael Castellano, a researcher with the United States Forest Service and the person responsible for identifying and categorizing fungi in need of special management. I find him in his modest ground-level office on the west side of campus, busy at his computer creating a handbook on endangered fungi in the region. It is a daunting task. Although already a world expert on truffles, Castellano faces the possibility of having to devote next year's research to extending his expertise in the genus *Ramaria*. Of the many fungi on the endangered list in the Pacific Northwest, twenty-four are *Ramaria*, and they pretty much all look alike — large, multibranched, coral-like, orange mushrooms. "It isn't easy," Castellano says of fungi identification. "They are cryptic, growing in the substrate, the bark, stumps, soil, sand. They're hard to deal with."

Ask scientists to peg the current understanding of fungi on a scale of one to ten, and they inevitably say one. Since new fungi are being discovered all the time, how can we begin to understand how an ecosystem fits together, much less manage it in the presence of clearcut logging until we have all the pieces of the puzzle? "We're low on the totem pole," Castellano says of science's understanding of the vast family of fungi. "If we have one million plants, we probably have ten million fungi. That's the order of magnitude."

Just as the forest industry denounced the spotted owl for tying up national forest lands in western Oregon — the annual cut dropped 81 percent in the five-year period ending in 1993 — fungi, too, have gained their share of enemies. Castellano confides that he has received reports of people removing rare conks — fungi that can reach the size of dinner plates, attached to the trunks of trees — in hopes that the area won't fall victim to timber-cutting restrictions. But such acts of vandalism are about as destructive as picking an apple in hopes of killing the tree — they do little to the unseen fungi. "It's silliness," Castellano points out. "The body of the organism is still there."

While he does not dismiss the economic impact of logging cut-backs on timber communities in the Pacific Northwest, he is quick to promote the benefits — practical, ecological, and aesthetic — of a biologically diverse world. Fungi are part of a larger quilt of life that helps to ensure healthy timber lands. "Do we want a diverse ecosystem or a Douglas fir monoculture?" he asks. "The forest is not just trees. It's thousands of organisms living together." Fungi are coming under intense study as sources of new medicines for everything from AIDS to cancer. Hospitals in Asia have long used mushroom extract containing "activated hexose-containing compound" to activate tumor-fighters in the immune system. Taking the cue, researchers at the University of California at Davis are testing the shiitake mushroom in the fight against prostate cancer, using extract made from partially mature spores that are treated with an enzyme and dried to avoid problems with patient allergies.

On the day I interview Castellano, a six-person crew, funded jointly through the United States Forest Service and Bureau of Land Management, is scouring an experimental forest at Cascade Head, west of Corvallis and north of Newport, for rare mushrooms. When the crew finds one, it will make a note of the surrounding vegetation, soil, and organic matter — clues to help find the fungi again elsewhere and possibly even remove it from the endangered list. Six people may be a woefully inadequate number to catalogue such a vast and complex world. But they are making a start, and it is worth noting that even the suggestion of the government hiring workers to find fungi to potentially put loggers out of business would be met by howls of protest from the forest industry in British Columbia, where there is little legislative protection for flora and fauna.

Throughout the Pacific Northwest, the scientific community

relies in large part on private clubs and enthusiasts to act as its nose in the field, sniffing out strange fungi and sending them in for identification. Every so often a collector gets lucky and takes credit for discovering a whole new species. One such person is Paul Kroeger, a self-trained mushroom expert, lecturer, and former president of the Vancouver Mycological Society, who pretty much embodies every idiosyncrasy you might attribute to a mycologist. I met him during a summer mushroom foray on the western slopes of Mount Elphinstone, site of three protected areas totaling just 370 acres on British Columbia's Sunshine Coast. Bushy of beard, soft spoken, and oozing acidic humor, he proceeds across the rainforest floor at a slug speed on his hands and knees. "There's really only one way to tell if a mushroom is poisonous," he offers, straight-faced. "Feed one to a lawyer and wait for the lawsuit."

Almost twenty years ago, Kroeger visited a friend's home on Saturna Island in the Gulf Islands, where he discovered an unusual mushroom growing on the carpet. He later discovered the same mushroom on an old chesterfield on the Musqueam Indian Reserve in South Vancouver and on a pair of discarded blue jeans in Cliff Gilker Park near Sechelt, not far from Mount Elphinstone. As the scientific community would eventually confirm, Kroeger had found a new species — *Melanotus textilis*, described in *Mushrooms Demystified* as "fruiting body yellow-brown to brown or cinnamon; stalk present, often darker, usually off-centre, curved, and slender." Since its official recognition, the mushroom has popped up all over, proving it was there all along, right under our noses. "It's been found in rolled-up work socks and Volkswagens," Kroeger says. "It even showed up in Scotland on a coconut-fibre door mat of Japanese origin."

Unique environmental conditions have transformed Mount Elphinstone into a fungi free-for-all, home to possibly hundreds of species. Since a wildfire swept through in the 1860s, logging has been limited to the removal several decades ago of dead cedars for shake blocks. Evolving naturally since then, the forest is today dominated by western hemlock and Douglas fir, the largest of which are several hundred years old and shielded against wildfires by their chunky bark.

Clearcut logging elsewhere on the Sunshine Coast hasn't been nearly so kind to fungi. "The forest industry is more interested in volume," Kroeger argues. "When you nuke the mycorrhizal fungi when you clearcut, you break up the whole web of life that is out there. It's so fundamental. Without the fungi, we wouldn't have the forest. It's a hidden world, complex beyond belief." Then Kroeger takes a deep breath and sarcastically corrects himself. "It's not a clearcut," he insists. "The land is being converted to second-growth, even-aged stands. The age being zero, of course."

As we move through the forest along an old logging skid road, Kroeger stops to grab a brittle, short-stemmed mushroom and puts it to the "Russula test," throwing it against an old cedar stump and watching it snap like white chalk. Then he picks up a small twig covered with what appear to be tiny eggs — a type of slime mold that at times appears to be moving. "I have these dreams where it is growing in the armpits of officials with the ministry of forests," he confesses. Just as the study of fungi is separate from the field of botany, some people believe slime molds are a world unto themselves. "There are some pretty crazy ideas about them. Some people say they come from comets. It's hard to disprove."

Even for experts, mushroom identification is no simple matter, let alone learning their scientific names as well. But to Kroeger it's all a matter of word association. The common puff ball, for example, is *Lycoperdon*. "Literally translated, wolf wind," he whispers. "Wolf farts."

For those who pick mushrooms with the idea of eating them, confusion can be lethal. In 1994 the provincial coroner's office enlisted Kroeger to investigate the death of a seventeen-year-old Nanaimo boy who had choked on his own vomit after consuming alcohol and mushrooms. Kroeger concluded the young man had eaten delirium-inducing *Amanita pantherina* mushrooms.

Among the most deadly of the mushrooms in the Pacific Northwest is the deathcap, or *Amanita phalloides*, which is responsible for more poisonings than any other mushroom. As recently as October 1997 a husband and wife were hospitalized after eating deathcaps found in their backyard in Vancouver, Washington. Commonly found beneath filbert and chestnut trees in Oregon but only recently discovered in Vancouver, B.C., the mushroom has white gills and often a yellow-green cap. The common symptoms of severe stomach pain, diarrhea, and liver damage do not begin to manifest themselves until six to twenty-four hours after ingestion and can lead to death.

Confusing matters further is the fact that many types of mushrooms are safe for wildlife consumption but unfit for humans. "We're a frail species," Kroeger remarks. "I've found bear scat with charcoal briquets in them." He remains confounded by the preoccupation with eating mushrooms, saying he would prefer that people learn about fungi from an ecological perspective rather than by using them to complement T-bones. "People needn't be blinded by their lust for food. But that's hard to get through to a person bubbling with enthusiasm. If you go out birdwatching, you're not popping off birds left, right, and centre and saying, 'Hey, are these good to eat?' With mushrooms, the real fascination is what's going on underground."

Still, the collection of wild mushrooms is an estimated $40-million-a-year business in the Pacific Northwest. The most popular varieties include the pine or matsutake, morel, shaggy parasol, hedgehog, coral tooth, chanterelle, truffle, and horn of plenty. Just as street gangs defend their turf, mushroom pickers are known to resort to guns to intimidate competitors at their favorite foraging spots. The fact that mushroom picking tends to occur in remote areas only encourages a sense of lawlessness in Canada and the U.S. alike. One fall in the Nass Valley of west-central British Columbia, the RCMP reported three separate incidents in which pickers pointed or fired rifles or shotguns to protect their claim for matsutake mushrooms, a prized export to Japan potentially worth thousands of dollars to each picker. In nearby Hazelton one season, the Mounties laid eight gun charges and dozens of alcohol- and narcotics-related counts after the community was beset by hundreds of mushroom pickers.

Although today's foray at Lake Hebo coincides with the start of deer-hunting season in Oregon, the truffle master is quick to alleviate our concerns. "I'm more comfortable hunting for truffles in deer season than mushrooming in matsutake country," Evans insists. Nonetheless, when I became lost en route to Lake Hebo earlier this morning, I chose to keep driving rather than seek assistance from a couple of gun-toting hunters walking along the roadside in search of prey. I have been accused of many foolish things in my life — most of them true — but stopping to ask directions from men with guns is not one of them.

As our group strikes out from Lake Hebo along a pioneer trail, blazed by settlers in 1854 to connect the Willamette and Tillamook valleys, our first find is poisonous, but a far evolutionary cry from a mushroom. A western rough-skinned newt, a member of the salamander family, is slithering across the ground just beneath my right boot. It is an alien-looking species with a bulbous head and a striking two-toned body — chocolate brown on the back, bright orange on the belly. "A friend of mine was driving down the road and had to stop," reflects truffler Kiko Denzer, a sculptor from Corvallis. "The road was covered with them." The newt walks about freely in the daytime, confident in knowing its skin carries enough toxin to potentially kill any animal that eats it, humans included.

Lake Hebo is little more than a pond with a few picnic tables, located 1,300 feet above sea level and surrounded by second-growth Sitka spruce and Douglas fir. Although most native trees in Oregon have an association with truffles, Douglas fir is an exceptionally good bet for truffle hunters year-round. And these people need all the help they can get. Unlike the search for mushrooms, which pop up all over the place as they flag down passersby with their assortment of sizes, shapes, and colors, truffle hunting can take years of skill, patience, and hands-on practice, with few identification books available for guidance. Just learning to tell a truffle from a "button," an early phase of an above-ground mushroom, is fraught with challenge. "It's like an Easter egg hunt," explains Evans, who takes credit for discovering five new species. "Truffles are like spices were in the Middle Ages — special and secretive."

Truffles also pack an aromatic wallop, with good reason. Because they grow underground, they rely on animals such as the flying squirrel to spread their spores so they can reproduce. The production of pungent aromas is nature's way of attracting those animals. "It's the truffle's way of telling the squirrel, 'Eat me, eat me,'" Evans says.

Some experienced hunters claim they can actually smell the presence of truffles the moment they walk into a forest. But the more common tracking method is to look for animal diggings or to start scratching around the roots of trees most closely associated with fungi. When we arrive at a suitable patch of forest after a five-minute walk, the trufflers split up and let the chase begin. Few are faster on the draw than my Internet contact, Wheeler, who works as an advertising copytaker at *The Oregonian*, Portland's daily newspaper. He is capable of typing 130 words a minute and is equally adept at poking around in the forest. He has so far found 115 species of truffles, perhaps 15 of which await confirmation as new species. The entire club has found more than 300 species of truffles in Oregon, one-tenth of them previously unknown, which only emphasizes the educational and scientific aspect of their recreation. "I've collected up to five pounds in one hour," Wheeler adds, putting them in a plastic gallon-sized container once used for dry catfood. "I've found truffles as deep down as ten inches."

While harvesting mushrooms may do no more harm to fungi than picking apples does to the tree, improper collection techniques, including extensive raking of the forest floor, can cause ecological harm. Society members are careful to disturb only small patches of soil and to replace the duff layer afterwards. Wicker picnic basket at her side, Pat Rollinson scratches the soil with prairie chicken efficiency, while a crafty Steller's jay swoops down to pick up discarded bits in her wake. Then she uproots a deer truffle, *Elaphomyces*, the size of a small brown button with warts. "All we're doing is sampling," explains the veteran forager. "Come back in three or four weeks and this will be healed over. But when whole areas are raked over, it irritates us."

Around noon, big dark clouds gather above the upper canopy of the rainforest, dimming the light on the understory and reducing the truffle hunters to mere silhouettes. Even people accustomed to hanging out in dark, dank places have their limits. "I don't know how we can possibly find a truffle," remarks Rollinson, her glasses reduced to two foggy orbs. Seconds later the skies open up and unleash a frightening alliance of wind and rain. As one wave after another whistles toward us, the truffle hunters decide to collect their booty and head home, hoping for drier weather on the next foray. At the same time, they realize that the rain fuels their passion and gives a future to their precious fungi.

CHAPTER 9

# The Interior
# Rainforest
*Seven Days Solo in*
*the Granby Wilderness*

SNOW HAS ARRIVED far too early in the southern Monashee Mountains. Still weeks before summer's end, the alpine tundra already shivers under a soggy blanket of slush as a biting wind cuts across the exposed scalp of Mount Scaia. There is a chill running through my confidence, too. I cannot help but wonder if my timing is all wrong for a solo, seven-day hike of the Granby Wilderness, the little-known, little-traveled Interior rainforest valley in southern British Columbia.

Preserved as a 400-square-kilometre provincial park only in 1995, the Granby is the last major unlogged watershed in the Boundary region, a transitional zone between the semi-arid Okanagan Valley and the mountainous West Kootenays. It is home to the Granby grizzly bear, the most isolated and most endangered population of grizzlies in the province. And it houses a rare pocket of Interior temperate rainforest that contains magnificent old-growth western red cedar, a species normally associated with the Pacific coast, a six-hour drive to the west.

There is much to entice me here, and just as much to keep me away. So freshly minted is the park that there are no road signs leading to it, no formal network of trails when I arrive. Not even an outhouse. And with no regular patrols by park wardens, there is no one to hear my cries, no one to offer assistance or go for help. Indeed, the Granby Wilderness is so unexplored that it is capable of swallowing me whole without so much as a bowel movement.

My friends and family believe I am afflicted with equal amounts of bravery and idiocy for attempting these sorts of feats, and they are usually half right. During a nineteen-day hike through the Mackenzie Mountains of the Northwest Territories in 1991 I came within a few gasps of drowning while crossing the Twitya River in a blizzard. A year later, during a six-week journey along the historic Stikine route to the Klondike, I generated an embarrassing airborne search-and-rescue mission when I became bogged down in the impossibly remote Stikine Plateau of northwestern British Columbia. That one hurt. An electronic locator transmitter — a device normally used on aircraft to signal the location of a crash — got me out of a tight squeeze. But I was left wondering: would I have done things differently had I not been carrying such an effective insurance policy in my backpack? One way or the other, I will now find the answer to that question, alone in the Granby Wilderness.

From the vantage point of Mount Scaia's 7,200-foot-high summit in the northeast corner of the park, the magnitude of my task unfolds neatly before me. I will hike due south, up and over a series of subalpine peaks and ridges marking the park's eastern boundary — Gunwad Mountain, Mount Young, and Mount Sloan. Then, rolling up my sleeves and taking one last deep breath, I will freefall 4,000 feet to the bottom of the Granby River Valley and hike out the park's southern entrance. From this lofty perspective the hike is a straight-line distance of almost fifty kilometres. But down there, amongst the cluttered montage of forest, deadfall, creeks, cliffs, and gullies, the route is much more circuitous and unpredictable. In fact, in the days ahead the only certainty is that there is no turning back. As I finish loading my backpack and cinching up my bootlaces, the dented tail-gate of my pickup truck is bouncing down the same badly pitted gravel access road that brought me here. The driver is David Simm, the Friends of the Granby Environmental Society member who accompanied me to Mount Scaia and who has now agreed to return to Grand Forks and leave my truck at the park's southern entrance to await my arrival. "Take care of yourself, Larry," he says with a final handshake. "It's going to be quite an adventure."

Clearly, this is not the time for second-guessing. The road to solace lies ahead, beyond the lingering shadows of self-doubt and the gauntlet of the Granby Wilderness. Under a billowy cover of clouds I take a compass reading on the peak of Gunwad Mountain and strike out across Scaia's soggy alpine meadows on a steady descent to the tree line. The terrain is littered with the scat and prints of grizzly bears, deer, and elk, but I must content myself with sightings of grouse, voles, and ground squirrels. Occasionally I also pick up faint and meandering animal trails, even a horse trail, but these inducements fill me with false hopes and waste my valuable energy before inevitably melting into the landscape with the wet snow. The steep hillsides combine with the short, wet vegetation to make treacherous hiking conditions. I slip hard on my back with banana-peel abruptness, and the beef jerky in my hand flies high into the air and into the brush, never to be seen or gnawed again.

Early evening finds me bushwhacking toward a small creek flowing through an armpit of a trench that separates Scaia from Gunwad. Conditions are poor for camping. The thick brush barely yields enough space for a tent. The wood on the ground burns grudgingly, while the dead lower limbs of the trees are too small and burn too quickly. With the approach of nightfall and inclement weather, I have little choice but to stay put. The skies grow slate gray and unleash an avalanche of wet, heavy snow. I struggle to make dinner, then crawl into my tent, only to find that water has gummed its way through the roof and collected in a pool on my sleeping bag. I go outside, brush off the snow, and move the tent further into the forest for protection, but that only makes matters worse. One of the aluminum poles snaps, the end sticking up painfully like a fractured leg and allowing moisture to pass through the roof. Placing a plastic bag over my sleeping bag for protection against the drip, drip, drip, I realize that what began as a challenging trek through scenic new parkland is fast becoming a test of emotional and physical survival.

Conditions make for a damp and restless night. By morning there is ice in my cooking pot and an inch and a half of new snow on the ground. The uphill journey is a struggle for balance on slopes still unthawed by the sun, while the thickets of brush shred my raingear as efficiently as scissors. Midway up the mountain I am buoyed to pick up a horse trail, only to lose it again closer to the top. By noon, my boots and wool pants sopping wet, the compass reading accurately directs me through a narrow pass across Gunwad's summit and on toward the next destination, Mount Young. An hour later, the first good news of the journey — a well-used horse trail merges in from the east. Although the horses' hooves have carved out deep muddy ruts, the trail is a welcome sight, a veritable freeway compared with the strain of bushwhacking.

Unfortunately, the weather is not nearly as favorable. By late afternoon the clouds turn ominous, the wet snow begins anew, and I steel myself for another long, wet night in the forest. Then — a mirage on the horizon? — the outline of an old Forest Service cabin emerges from the flurry of snowflakes. Under these rugged circumstances it is as welcome as a five-star hotel. Not much bigger than an ordinary living room, the cabin boasts two cots with foam mattresses, a woodstove, a clothesline, a table, candles, matches, dry paper, kindling and firewood, an axe, soap, paper plates, and a rain jacket. Abandoned provisions include macaroni, sugar, rice, and even chewing tobacco, bug dope, and spray for jock itch.

Although the cabin is maintained by a backcountry horse club based in the West Kootenay community of Nakusp, the dominant clientele is hunters. One inscription on the wall reads: "88 Sept. 04. Saw one grizzly with two cubs, two billy goats and some deer." Another: "Arrived 1500 hours, 93 Aug. 30, en route to Mt. Sloan, with 6 horses, 4 pack horses. Left Sept. 5. Saw one grizzly and lots of deer."And then there is the cabin fauna. As the room warms with a stove fire, a disgusting army of flies, each the size of a jelly bean, emerges from the woodwork in a sort of groggy stasis. Later that evening, when I crawl into my sleeping bag after digesting a hot rehydrated dinner, a mouse scurries across my exposed left arm, ensuring that my sleep in the cabin is no more restful than my first night in the forest.

The next morning, reason for optimism. The sun is poking through the clouds, my clothes are dry, my belly full, and the trail easy to follow. For an hour and a half I struggle up a steep incline, sidestepping the trench of mud created by horse hooves, en route to the summit of Mount Young. Then, on the side of the trail in the subalpine zone, a wisp of smoke. Humans. First contact. The campsite of Frank Kacsinko, a chemical engineer from Trail, and Leo Langergraber, a machine-shop operator from Grand Forks, a couple of good ol' boys getting an early start on a two-week mule-deer hunt.

I suspected someone was up here. Late yesterday afternoon I heard a muffled gunshot and concluded it came from hunters. But Langergraber tells a different tale from the one I imagined. The snowstorm took the two men by surprise, and they became separated. Disoriented and with no landmarks to guide him, Langergraber traveled all the way back down the mountain on horseback to the cabin in search of his friend before he realized his mistake and turned around. Conditions deteriorated to the point that the two men had to fire gunshots to find each other in the whiteout. "You have to be careful in this country," concedes Kacsinko, noting that just a week ago it was below freezing. "The weather is unpredictable."

The ordeal safely behind them, the two men are friendly, inquisitive, and accommodating, offering me a plate of bacon and eggs cooked on a greasy skillet heavily spiced with seasoning salt. There are also buns, pears, and — as Kacsinko reveals only after I've eaten them — sausages made with black-bear meat. I enjoy the warmth of their fire but am discouraged to see that they have used a chainsaw to hack up the park's slow-growing alpine trees. That is the environmental price to be paid for an absence of management in the Granby Wilderness, a place where hunters with horses are capable of hauling up machinery and gasoline and where the phrase "no-trace camping" is in nobody's vocabulary. Yet they seem more concerned that I might encourage more traffic to the area. "It's all virgin country," says Kacsinko. "Few people from the city come here. You gonna put it on the map?"

Langergraber sizes up my thick calves and choice of hiking shorts despite the chilly temperatures. Then, rather than offering a dismissive comment about the sanity of my expedition, he admits to more than a little jealousy at my sense of adventure. He has been hunting since 1968, as much for the lifestyle and horsemanship as the venison. "I live an uneventful life," he allows, "but I do like wilderness travel."

That night I struggle to make camp alone, several hours away, in a light drizzle on the south side of Mount Young. That infernal finicky tent. It no longer sits properly to drain off the rain. I am forced to improvise, taping a wooden splint to the broken metal rod to give the tent shape. Wedged into a small stand of firs, it is enough to keep me reasonably dry. Still, sleep remains elusive. There is too much to occupy my thoughts. The tent. The route ahead. The presence of grizzly bears. My apprehension isn't helped by a couple of unidentifiable, high-pitched animal screams somewhere in the inky darkness, enough to make me venture outside the tent and rekindle the campfire.

The next morning the mountains are choking on thick, low cloud. I delay my journey until early afternoon, entertained by a brief visit from a magnificent mule-deer buck, before deciding to press on and follow the edge of a steep, rocky ridge in visibility of eighty yards. It is an eerie experience — mists swirling around, ground squirrel burrows excavated by grizzlies, the only sound my own heavy breathing and the crunch of leather soles on rock and heather. After two hours of walking, Mount Sloan's 7,500-foot summit poses a formidable challenge dead ahead. But rather than attempt a suicidal hike up and over, I follow an animal path leading around the peak's ragged shoulders at the base of a rockslide. Three mule deer feeding on a lush meadow watch my approach nervously, then bound away into the spruce forest as though propelled by pogo sticks.

Nightfall finds me making camp near the ridge, scrounging for snow to melt for water and struggling to set up my damaged tent in a pelting downpour. The tent is located near a well-used animal trail — an unwise move, but unavoidable given the uneven terrain, approaching nightfall, and my exhaustion. When sleep finally comes, I dream first of being approached by a pack of wolves and having to punch the Alpha male in the snout when he comes too close. Then I dream of lying in the tent as the shadow of a huge grizzly passes overhead . . . and thinking I really shouldn't have eaten that bear sausage.

Perhaps it is all some kind of a test, for the next morning the weather breaks like a bad fever. Finally the world is mine to behold. The alpine ridge looms like the rocky spine of a prostrate giant. The vistas are no less immense, almost oceanic in proportion, the mountains receding into the horizon, one emerald wave after another on an undulating sea. And far below to the west, my first glimpse of the rainforest of the Granby River Valley. It is nothing more than a pinch in the landscape from this height, but it is the fluid wilderness highway that will lead me home.

The sudden clearing of weather allows me to reflect on the unusual realm I am about to enter. Despite appearing to be an ecosystem swept off course and deposited here by the vagaries of nature, the Granby is a true temperate rainforest, as authentic as those of Clayoquot Sound or the Queen Charlotte Islands. It is part of the Interior cedar-hemlock zone, the rarest temperate rainforest in British Columbia, representing less than 5 percent of the provincial land base. Interior forests feature a greater diversity of tree species than those on the coast because they are subject to more wildfires, which allow greater growth of first-stage deciduous plants. The Granby Valley is an example of this sort of diverse and complex landscape. Besides the old-growth cedar and hemlock in the valley bottoms, there are stands of Engelmann spruce and subalpine fir at higher elevations, changing to drier Douglas fir and ponderosa pine as one moves southward to the Canada-United States border.

From the top-of-the-world security of Mount Young, it is an intimidating thing to plunge headfirst down into the Granby's suffocatingly thick forests in hopes of emerging safe and sound the better part of a day later. I am only too aware that in the impenetrable darkness of the forest, in the absence of a trail and an emergency locator transmitter, any serious injury could prove fatal. I may never be found. But the break in the rainclouds tells me there won't be a better time than now. With a hard swallow and a final adjustment of my pack I take the first tentative steps downhill.

The route begins easily enough, a dry, south-facing slope, sparsely treed, with only minimal bushwhacking. But before long the forest thickens until I am inching my way over fallen logs, fighting tangled brush, ploughing through bogs, and scrambling across precipitous rockfalls. There are camping supplies I have inadvertently left behind — three bricks of cheese in my fridge, my drinking cup and leather belt in the truck — but the truly important items always seem to make it into the pack. At this moment they include my carbon-based water filter, which allows me to suck up fluids from the most turbid of puddles without fear of intestinal retribution. Still, hunkered down beside this pathetic watering hole, columns of mosquitoes feeding off my sweaty exposed flesh, a knife attached menacingly to my right hip with a strand of rope, I fear the line between man and animal has become dangerously blurred.

Just as I think the ordeal will never end, the forest gradually begins to thin and become drier, and the thick cover of evergreens is replaced by the warmth of pine trees sprinkled across an old burn site. I am buoyed to see the Granby River for the first time, and, relieved to see it funneling in the right direction — southward to Grand Forks, the Kettle River, and the once-mighty Columbia River in eastern Washington.

I arrive at the riverbank half an hour later, finally free of the forest's gnarly grip and soothed by a blue pastel sky. Instead of following the river, I make the mistake of following yet another false lead, hiking a marked trail that traverses diagonally from the riverbank up a steep slope. By the time it becomes covered in deadfall and is obviously going the wrong way, I have wasted considerable energy, fighting my way uphill in the hot afternoon. There is nothing to do but struggle dejectedly back to the valley bottom, wade across the knee-high river, and set up camp on an exposed gravel bar. There I bathe in the river, dry out beside a robust campfire, and prepare for an explosion of stars while kicking back a well-deserved tug of rum reserved for medicinal purposes only.

Although the challenge of navigating this uncharted wilderness is over, I still face a two-day journey through the narrow valley floor to the south entrance of the park. And as I quickly discover, the rough going has only started. True, the patches of old-growth rainforest are inspiring. The largest western red cedars grow to thirty feet in circumference, spared from forest fires all these centuries by the dripping humidity and dim sunlight on the valley floor. To walk among the legs of these botanical dinosaurs, ferns the size of bamboo rakes poking up through their toes, is a wilderness hiker's dream. But for every open pocket of old-growth there are long stretches of younger forest in which the understory is mined with deadfall and choked with vine maple, devil's club, red alder. To avoid these sections requires wading through the river or, when the water narrows and deepens, detouring uphill over steep, slippery bluffs. On one particularly nasty section I hear a loud, strange noise. I stop and look up at the treetops to see if they are creaking in the wind, but the afternoon is dead calm. Then the noise again, and this time there is no doubt: it's the long, loud bawling of a bear cub, perhaps twenty yards away and obviously feeling threatened by my presence.

Threatened by loss of habitat from clearcutting and human encroachment, a population of perhaps forty grizzlies exists in the southern Monashees. Deprived of the rich salmon runs enjoyed by their fat coastal cousins and forced to subsist on marginal, mostly dry habitat, the Granby grizzly is the runt of its species, not much bigger than a medium-sized black bear. Barry Brandow, a professional hunting guide for the past twenty years in the Monashees, told me he has spotted thirty to forty grizzlies, their coats ranging from dark brown to ash blonde. The bears enjoy the gut-pile residue from a successful mule-deer hunt and the tasty ground squirrels that honeycomb the subalpine meadows. But black huckleberries — so sweet they are commercially harvested in portions of the Cascade Mountains — are what really get the grizzlies through the winter, and when the crop fails, as it is prone to do in the hot southern Interior, so does the bear population. "They're sort of always on the edge, marginal even when they get enough food," Brandow reflected. "I remember one grizzly killed before my time, a mature female, about twenty-eight years of age. The hunter was able to pick it up with both hands." Now protected from hunting, the grizzlies' best hope for long-term survival in the southern Interior is the Granby Wilderness, along with a second newly protected area to the southeast, Gladstone Provincial Park.

But right now, standing in the middle of a dark forest on the edge of a precipitous cliff, I am the one who feels threatened. Talking calmly, I continue to move slowly southward, glancing frequently over my shoulder, until the danger has passed. But I'm not completely out of the forest: a couple of hours later I slip badly while crossing a log and pull the muscle of my left calf. The pain is excruciating; at home I'd almost certainly take a couple of days off work and seek out a physiotherapist. Alone in the wilderness, with no help in sight, I can only watch as my calf blackens and swells up like a ripe melon and limp my way back to civilization. But that's only half of it. Instead of toughening up with each passing day, my forty-something body is falling apart, piece by piece. Bruised shoulders. Red welts where the pack rubs against my sides. Throbbing legs. And vertebrae that behave like the springs of an old car each time I put on my 60-pound backpack. When a turkey vulture makes a low and deliberate sweep overhead, I take it personally.

Early the next morning I rejoice at finding a few faded yellow ribbons on the forest floor, marking a twelve-kilometre trail hacked out by the Granby Wilderness Society and leading to my vehicle, parked at the Forest Service campsite near the south end of the park. With the major natural obstacles now behind me, and proceeding under sunny skies, my progress is good, despite my calf injury. The forests become drier, the understory thinner, the bordering mountains smaller and rockier. The river undergoes a transformation, too: one minute it rages out of control through spectacular, sheer-rock canyons; the next it sleeps peacefully in a series of deep, translucent pools that are home to trout and the speckled dace, a rare species of fish found in the province only in the Granby and Kettle rivers.

With the best access for vehicles and with a maintained trail that is mostly flat and easy to hike, this area is the one small corner of the Granby Wilderness that most visitors experience. A few hundred come every year, and, judging from the names on the trailhead register, they hail from all over the world. Ironically — some would say tragically — these people are not visiting the park at all. When Granby park was created, officials pegged the southern boundary about five kilometres up the trail from the Forest Service campsite. Worse yet, the British Columbia forests ministry has plans to allow logging of 4,700-acre Traverse Creek, thereby ruining the wilderness experience for all who visit. It is just one of many logging battles still being waged, so soon after the initial euphoria over the protection of the Granby, by conservationists and the Sinixt Nation, which claims aboriginal title to this territory. Clearcut logging is also pushing toward the skinny middle portion of the park from Burrell Creek on the east and Goatskin Creek on the west.

As the trailhead and campsite finally come into view, marking the end of my expedition, I remain amazed that a wilderness as raw and vast as Granby has remained so isolated in much-traveled southern

British Columbia. But that isolation is also cause for concern. Would the provincial government consider allowing logging at the entrance to some of its better-known parks — Garibaldi, Manning, Golden Ears — which are closer to urban populations? I don't think so. But as the little-known Granby is about to discover, behind the dark veil of public ignorance, the unimaginable becomes possible.

# CHAPTER 10

# On Your Knees for Alaska Man

*Prince of Wales Island's
Limestone Caves*

TO THIS DAY, Harvey Wilcox beats himself up. It wasn't enough that he stumbled upon the cave containing the greatest archaeological site in Alaska or Canada or anywhere else along the vertical spine of rainforest extending 2,500 miles along the Pacific coast of North America. He's still hard on himself for forgoing the opportunity to be the first to look inside that cave, to stand at the threshold of history and sift his fingers through the sediments of time, to set his eyes upon ancient bones that continue to reshape theories about the first settlement of North America. That he gave up the chance in order to rush back for camp gruel is what really sickens him. "We wanted to look at it," he insists with a measure of humor. "But we were staying at a logging camp and the cook was a real bitch and didn't like it when you were late for dinner. We had to run."

Wilcox was employed as a contract logging engineer for the United States Forest Service on that eventful hot July afternoon in 1993, working alone on the northwestern tip of Prince of Wales Island in southeast Alaska. He was studying the rugged old-growth terrain to determine the economic viability of a proposed logging road route. That's when he made his first discovery — a black-bear den beneath the roots of an ancient cedar tree, the entrance marked by a wide swath of flattened grass and brush. "It was like he'd taken a lawn mower and mowed everything for 200 feet in all directions. When I first walked up I said, 'Wow, this is one pissed-off bear.'" That's when he fetched two biologists working on an environmental assessment of the same logging road route, and they returned to the den. "I took a flashlight and crawled down in it. But the bear wasn't home, as far as I could tell."

Investigation completed, they started to leave for camp through a cut in the forest when Wilcox looked uphill, more than 100 yards away, and remarked on a hole in the mountain. "It looked almost like a mine, not a natural cave. It looked artificial." He badly wanted to check it out. So did the biologists. But it was already late afternoon and camp was still an hour away.

Wilcox left the area confident he would return for a closer inspection. But it didn't work out that way. That job would be left to others. His duties never allowed him to return to the cave. In fact, the next time he heard much about it was through a letter from his employer four years later — pretty much the only recognition he can expect — congratulating him for discovering such an important archaeological site. He didn't know whether to pinch himself or kick himself in the ass. He still doesn't. "Damn, why didn't I go over there? All I had was a little bitty penlight, but I have always wondered, 'If I had looked in, would I have seen all that?'"

Among the mysteries waiting inside the cave that day was Alaska

Man. At least that's what I call him. Scientists have been slow at getting around to a formal christening since discovering his chewed-up,
covered-over remains. I suppose there is no hurry. After all, he died
almost 10,000 years ago, barely in his twenties. When discovered on
July 4, 1996, covered by ancient sediments in a small chamber thirty
feet inside the cave, all that remained of him was three vertebrae, a
partial right pelvis, and a mandible, more angular than that of con-
temporary native Americans, in two fragments. His teeth were cavity-
free and in good shape, but they were missing the four incisors and
showing extensive wear. The finding is typical of a gritty shellfish diet
and consistent with an isotope bone analysis showing that Alaska
Man lived off marine life, not a land-based diet of terrestrial meat. He
lived in a cool, dry climate that followed the climax of the last ice age
17,000 years ago. And he traveled by water past areas of coastal refu-
gia that had escaped the weight of the great glaciers — a landscape of
tundra, willow, and spruce, species that preceded today's temperate
rainforest.

Pretty much everything else about Alaska Man's life is open to
speculation. It is tempting to conclude he died a violent death consistent with our view of prehistoric people's live-hard, die-young lifestyle. Evidence of carnivore gnawing on his pelvis suggests that he was
attacked by one of the monstrous brown bears — grizzlies to anyone
outside Alaska — that once roamed Prince of Wales Island and that
he was dragged inside the cave to be eaten at leisure. But it is equally
possible that he died from unrelated causes — disease, warfare, an
accident — and was buried in the cave, or that his bones were dragged
inside by an opportunistic scavenger.

What we can say with certainty is that Alaska Man is only part
of a much bigger picture emerging from within the filthy bowels of
On Your Knees Cave. Since the discovery of the cave, scientists have
turned up a prolific assortment of mammalian bones, which together

provide a continuous history of life here dating back 40,000 years. It is a record that adds immeasurably to the theory that, yes, North America was populated by people following the Bering land bridge — the umbilical cord that once linked Siberia with Alaska. But no, these first inhabitants did not travel overland along an ice-free corridor east of Canada's Rocky Mountains, but by watercraft, following southward along coastal, ice-free areas of Alaska's Alexander Archipelago.

In a state known for scenic superlatives, the cave discovered by Wilcox is one of the most nondescript places you could find. It is a dud even among spelunkers, lacking the showy features one might find in, say, Carlsbad Caverns in New Mexico, or even elsewhere on Prince of Wales Island, including El Capitan, the longest cave in Alaska, with more than two miles of mapped passageway and a 624-foot drop, the deepest vertical pit in the United States. The cave more closely resembles a fissure, featuring two small entrances connected by 223 feet of horseshoe-shaped passageway burrowing more than twenty-five feet below the surface. According to Timothy Heaton, the University of South Dakota paleontologist who eventually uncovered its titanic importance, the cave is "a dirty little crawl, low, tight, and wet," one of the most difficult caves he has worked in.

Today the place is known to a euphoric scientific community as On Your Knees Cave, and the surrounding pocket of old-growth western hemlock and Sitka spruce rainforest is protected as "semi-remote recreation" under a revised land-management plan for the Tongass National Forest. To stand outside the cave where Alaska Man met his match is to put yourself at the crossroads of time: you can look back thousands of years, to a time when the first humans fanned out across this continent — the true aboriginal founders, not disoriented European latecomers — or you can look forward to see the vulnerability of this fragile, fractured landscape under the influences of industrial civilization. Given the patience of history, one senses that greater urgency lies ahead. In less than half a century, industrial America has chopped, hacked, and carved a frightening hole out of the rainforests of southeast Alaska. Nowhere is the devastation more pronounced than on Prince of Wales Island, the third largest in the United States after Alaska's Kodiak Island and the Big Island of Hawaii.

It is no coincidence that Prince of Wales is situated within one of North America's most extensive limestone deposits of calcium carbonate — known as karst — an area exceeding 700 square miles or 11 percent of the Ketchikan area of the Tongass National Forest. These carbonate rocks originated more than 400 million years ago as marine reef and lagoon deposits near the equator, rafting northward aboard oceanic plates that eventually collided with the continent off southeast Alaska. Not only are the deposits extensive, but they are exceptionally pure—up to 99.46 percent calcium carbonate, according to a chemical analysis of samples obtained from northern Prince of Wales Island. Combined with heavy rainfalls of naturally acidic water, the conditions are perfect for the creation of a vast subterranean network of caves, shafts, sinkholes, and underground streams. The carbonate also creates prime conditions for growing big trees; not only does the limestone allow drainage of the extensive rainfall in the area — up to 240 inches per year — but cracks in the bedrock give tree roots a good foothold against the powerful winter winds.

Unfortunately, the role of logging in this relationship is more parasitic than symbiotic. Clearcutting has caused irreparable damage to this fragile ecosystem, allowing the thin, nutrient-rich soils that overlay the bedrock to dry out or wash away in the heavy rains. As well, logging slash and sediment find their way into caves, where they stain or damage fragile features and clog passages. In doing so, they cripple the caves' unique capacity for turning vinegar into wine. Studies show that the water entering these features from, say, an overlying bog is especially acidic, with pH levels in the range of 2.4 to 5.8. But by the time this water filters through the carbonate and emerges from the caves, it shows a reading of 7.5 to 9.0. Combined with the ability of caves to moderate water temperature and flow, it's understandable that karst systems are up to ten times more productive for aquatic life. Logging also compromises the island's karst, crucial to a wide diversity of life forms. Five species of bats use the caves as roost sites, moving just far enough inside to avoid freezing temperatures on the outside. Deer, bear, wolves, and small furbearers use the caves or cave entrances for resting or denning. And dozens of species of invertebrates can be found in the twilight zone between light and dark near the cave entrance.

The fragile link between forest and cave is not an obvious one. But it has consumed Jim Baichtal since he arrived here as a forest geologist with the United States Forest Service in 1990, just three years after the first formal mapping and exploration of Prince of Wales' caves. Equal parts educator, scientist, and wilderness gladiator, he's also about as close as you get to a modern-day cave man. And that is saying something in America's Last Frontier, where it is alleged of the men that "the odds are good, but the goods are odd." A local radio station broadcaster once called Baichtal "a brick," but that description is far too limiting. He is built of old-growth fibre — a broad and beefy trunk, limbs strong enough to support a nest of eagles, and a beard as long and bushy as cat-tail moss. You could say, too, that his feet are firmly on the ground. When he walks through the forest with his laced, calf-high, leather boots, he leaves bear-sized depressions in the topsoil and assumes the appearance of the mythical Sasquatch of the Pacific Northwest.

Baichtal cusses and chews Red Man tobacco. At quitting time he can be found holding two beer bottles — an empty one, for spitting, in his left hand; a full one, for guzzling, in his right — and may one never be mistaken for the other. He enjoys the company of a good woman — Karen Petersen, assistant city clerk in Thorne Bay — and together they own the Riptide Liquor Store, "where we offer a wide variety of spirits at a fair price." He likes to read, mostly about the history and nature of the North. He thrives on a hearty belly laugh and can be brought to tears of laughter by a joke. And he maintains a healthy passion for country music. When I lead off with the words to the quirky Jerry Reed hit, "She got the gold mine . . ." he is quick to finish with divorcee precision, ". . . and I got the shaft."

Baichtal is also a mountain man, the consummate hunter, the ultimate carnivore. Dinner at his house consists of steaks from barren-ground caribou and Sitka black-tailed deer and two types of black-bear sausage. His modest two-story townhouse is the one with the tangle of antlers out front and the portable smoker exuding the sweet, warm aroma of alder wood and coho salmon. Inside, the walls are adorned with the wilderness prints of artist Paul Calle and the velvety pelts and mounted busts of wildlife that got in the way of his traps or rifles. He wears blue jeans and suspenders, and a silver belt buckle the size of a cake plate confirms his lifetime membership in the National Rifle Association.

Never one to miss the path less traveled, Baichtal even builds his own muskets — long, heavy black-powder affairs capable of blowing a hole the size of a golf ball through a bull moose at fifty paces. He can regale visitors for hours with hunting stories, like the time he was hiding in the tall grass and shot a big male black bear, then watched, horrified, as the wounded beast turned and charged straight at him before crumpling dead at his feet. "When you shoot those things, you realize the Natives had an advantage," he says. "I could shoot four or five arrows to one reloading of the flintlock." While Baichtal enjoys the challenge of the hunt, he is quick to point out he does not kill for idle pleasure and ensures that every scrap of the animal is used. This is a man who has not bought meat in a store in twelve years and who maintains a collection of bear-penis swizzle sticks. "The bigger ones come off the bigger bears," he says with a sly smile. "That's all I'm going to say."

Baichtal is also a civil servant who has gone underground in the name of conservation, to minimize the destructive impact of clearcut logging on the hidden world of karst. In some areas of Prince of Wales Island, up to 80 percent of the old-growth timber on carbonate bedrock has been harvested, more than twice the level of logging on non-carbonate landscapes. The island's Staney Creek area features an elevated 267-acre patch of forest — known locally as Masada — within a larger clearcut exceeding 9,500 acres, dating from the 1970s. This moonscape is an enduring symbol of past logging practices, since replaced by a federal policy of clearcuts averaging thirty acres. "Let's face it," Baichtal says. "The landscape has been raped by timber harvesting. There's nothing more you can say about it."

The federal Cave Resources Protection Act of 1988 brought about a measure of protection from logging on federal lands — as evidenced by On Your Knees Cave. But the legislation still fails to recognize the complete karst world, an ecosystem that is much more than a number of isolated caves. It is a complex, interconnected world that requires protection in its entirety. To emphasize his point, Baichtal tried an experiment to reveal the complex hydrology of karst systems. He put fluorescent dye in Thunder Falls Cave during the dry summer of 1991 and watched it emerge almost two miles away and thirty-two days later. He tried the same thing at Beaver Falls — not once, but three times — and still doesn't know where the dye went.

Baichtal's office has surveyed as much as 6,000 acres of rainforest per year for karst in advance of timber sales. To the trained eye, the landscape makes a poor poker face: well-drained areas of carbonate bedrock are dominated by Sitka spruce and western hemlock, the wetter, poorly drained areas by yellow and western red cedar. When a cave or sinkhole is found, a minimum thirty-yard no-logging buffer is placed around the entrance to help protect against windthrow. Exceptional areas of karst require stronger measures: about half of a sixty-acre harvest unit was removed from harvesting after the discovery of seven shafts that became known as Seven Dwarfs Cave.

As for On Your Knees Cave, its discovery is playing an important role not just in the greater scientific community, but right here on Prince of Wales Island, focusing international attention on the sort of problems that have bedeviled Baichtal for years. Still, the cave is far from a household name. News of the discoveries being unearthed here has been slow to reach the outside world. As the first journalist lucky enough to get inside the cave for a first-hand look, I am beginning to understand why. To get here, I drove two long days from Vancouver through the Interior of British Columbia to the northwestern logging and fishing port of Prince Rupert. I hopped a float plane for a forty-five-minute flight north to the Alaskan cruise-ship terminal of Ketchikan, where I boarded another float plane the next morning for a twenty-minute flight west to Thorne Bay, on Prince of Wales Island. There, waiting at the dock in his government-issue, extended-cab pickup truck, was Baichtal, who drove me almost three hours over gravel logging roads to a public dock on northern Prince of Wales Island. And we are not there yet. As Baichtal launches his *Boston Whaler* off the public dock and motors out toward the still, blue expanse of Sumner Strait — the last leg of my circuitous journey — I realize I am blessed with one of those rare sunny summer Alaskan afternoons that make you forget just how unlikeable this place can be on a blustery winter day.

Coronation Island looms enticingly on the horizon, last stop before the open Pacific and the Japanese island of Honshu, some 4,500 lonely miles to the west. Coho salmon, smooth stones skipping across the water surface, hint at the bounty below the surface. Two humpback whales feed on a school of needlefish, their backs breaking the clear, blue cellophane of ocean in neat unison. A Steller sea lion is on the hunt, threading its way through a forest of bull kelp. And a raft of pigeon guillemots bob calmly under the warm, reflective glow of a limestone cliff. "I love the shoreline," says Baichtal, pulling up to a small shell-and-gravel beach. "It's incredibly dynamic where the two worlds collide."

Just as the landscape has evolved from tundra to rainforest over the years, oceanic conditions too have changed around Prince of Wales Island. At the height of the last glaciation, the sea level was 300 to 400 feet lower than it is today. As the glaciers melted, the sea level rose, effectively drowning artifacts of tremendous importance. It reached as high as twenty feet above modern levels 10,000 years ago during Alaska Man's brief existence here on Prince of Wales Island. Today, On Your Knees Cave is located 450 feet above sea level; the trail leading there is a thirty-minute goat climb through an old-growth forest, which, given the archaeological circumstances, is the youngest feature of the landscape. For Alaska Man, the route was nothing more than a brisk walk, a combination of tundra and open forest. For Baichtal, it is a struggle. Suffering from a cold, he labors his way up and over the deadfall and stumps with the grace of a wounded elephant. We arrive at our destination dirty and sweaty, but no match for the filthy excavation crew that is busy hauling and screening sediments excavated from a foxhole dug just outside the entrance.

"This is a tough place to work logistically," confirms Jim Dixon, the curator of archaeology at the Denver Museum of Natural History, sporting a stubble beard, jeans, T-shirt, and white running shoes. "You saw the trail." The crew, which includes two representatives of the local Tlingit tribe from Klawock and Craig, has set up a yurt, an octagon-shaped tent on a wooden platform with an oil stove, as its base camp. Water is hauled up in plastic buckets from a shallow well dug from a gorge 100 yards below the encampment. Brush has been cleared away from the cave entrance, and a big old-growth cedar — spared the loggers' chainsaw — has regrettably been chopped down by scientists to allow for helicopter supply deliveries on a sling through the upper canopy.

On this particular afternoon the excavation crew is not alone. Although the cave is largely a secret to the outside world, its location is well known on northern Prince of Wales. When residents make unannounced visits to the cave, they are inevitably accommodated, part of the process of keeping the local community informed and supportive. "It's pretty neat," confirms Joe Sebastian, a commercial salmon troller on an outing with his son and daughter. "We live within five miles of something internationally significant. But this is the tip of the iceberg. This place is studded with caves, all the way up and down the coast."

In a community that derives its living from the land and the sea, there are few hardened positions on logging. But there must be limits, and the discovery of Alaska Man is helping to focus the debate. "This will bring new attention to the area," Sebastian says. "We're trying to find a new balance for the future. You can chop a tree down fast or slow, but once it's gone, it will take hundreds of years to grow it back." He is also hopeful that the discovery of Alaska Man will help to resolve the walk-or-canoe question regarding the first people to follow the Bering land bridge. And as someone who spends much of his life on the seas, Sebastian is forgiven for harboring a bias. "To me, it's fairly obvious. Would you want to come by boat or walk along rough terrain with all that gear? All aboriginal people of the West Coast are water-oriented."

The bones being discovered in On Your Knees Cave are so old

they push the outer limits of radiocarbon dating. There is a black-bear tibia dated to 41,600 years; a brown-bear femur to 35,365 years; a marmot incisor to 32,900 years; two ringed seals, one to 13,690 years, the other to 20,670 years, spanning the last ice age; a red fox to 11,276 years; a deer to 5,250 years. Some of these bones are from sick or old creatures that struggled into the cave and died, while other bones come from animals that were killed or scavenged elsewhere, then dragged inside by predators. The total assemblage is outdone by one other bone — a marmot tooth, dated to at least 44,500 years — at Devil's Canopy Cave, nearby on Prince of Wales Island.

The bears are part of another mystery that extends throughout the Alexander Archipelago. As though Mother Nature was forced to send two quarreling species to their separate rooms, the brown bears got exclusive rights to Admiralty, Baranof, and Chichagof islands in the north; the black bears got the south, including Prince of Wales Island. Based on their studies of bone specimens dated through radiocarbon testing, however, scientists know that both brown and black bears co-existed on Prince of Wales as long ago as 40,000 years and as recently as 6,000 years. Why the brown bears vanished from Prince of Wales, along with the red fox, caribou, and marmot, remains unknown.

Equally confounding are the different foraging strategies used by brown and black bears thousands of years ago. Brown-bear bones have been found at all elevations on Prince of Wales Island, while the black-bear bones exist mainly in coastal caves. However, an isotope analysis of their bones shows that the brown bears had both a land-based and marine diet, suggesting they ate salmon or patrolled the tidal zone in search of food part of the time, whereas the black bears were exclusively terrestrial, feeding on plants.

Whatever the answers to these mysteries, one important finding has emerged: if the Alexander Archipelago could sustain large carnivores such as brown bears on a marine diet so long ago, it could support humans, too. While screening the sediments from On Your Knees Cave, excavation crews have also unearthed several cultural artifacts: razor-sharp microblades of chert inserted into bone points; and obsidian, a black form of volcanic glass, possibly acquired through trading with natives as far away as Mount Edziza up the Stikine River in northwestern British Columbia. The cool, stable environment inside the caves — equal to the annual mean outside temperature — is perfect for preserving artifacts with the efficiency of a climate-controlled museum. For the same reasons, however, the caves remain extremely vulnerable to disturbance, not just by logging, but by ignorant human intruders. Even a handprint can last decades on a piece of ancient flowstone. A careless bump from a caver's hardhat can destroy a karst feature that took nature hundreds of years to create — the same effect as clearcutting old-growth timber. Still, visitors have an innate desire to take a piece of cave history home with them. Notes Baichtal, "People don't understand. They have this need to do it, to put it on the window sill at home."

In the sediments of On Your Knees Cave — layer upon layer of organic soil, clay, sand, and till — scientists are searching not just for artifacts, but for pollen and other indicators of climate change over the millennia, the transformation from tundra to rainforest. "This tunnel is like a life-line," Dixon says. "We want to link the record of the cave with the larger environment outside. I want to know how this region helped mold early American cultures. Whoever they were, they set the stage. We want to get at the roots, to understand them. This will tell us where the rainforest came in. It will show the antiquity of the rainforest." Then he adds with conviction, "This is turning out to be one hell of a cave."

Approaching the cave with trepidation, Baichtal and I crouch down to avoid hitting our heads and slowly waddle just inside the entrance. Pointing to a cramped tunnel leading to our left he says: "Forty feet down that passage is where the human remains were found. Imagine, something so subtle, yet so significant. A window to the past." Then he looks over his left shoulder, to his own world unfolding behind him, and tries to make that 10,000-year leap in time to the world Alaska Man knew before entering this cave for the last time. It is a distance more easily bridged by a man who has remained close to the land, who has long viewed the wilderness as his home, who has fought and narrowly won his own battles with the bears that roam this island. "This was tundra, the climate drier and colder, maybe willow and black spruce, too, up here," Baichtal offers, sizing up the landscape. "You can just imagine hunting along the shoreline, then looking up and seeing the cave, a place to survive, a place of refuge."

Then he stops to ponder the details of what really happened, what caused these bones to become strewn in this tiny crawl space. As he sees it, Alaska Man carried a spear — the chert tips hint at it — and either through misfortune or inexperience picked on the wrong bear on the wrong day. The classic tale of the hunter turned hunted. "Remember, these were big brown furry fuckers, not the little black pussycats that we have today. Things like that happen." Which leads to one final anthropological observation. "I'll tell you one thing, anybody who stuck one of those bears in the ass with a sharp stick had big balls."

CHAPTER 11

# The Sky
# Loggers

*Harvesting by Helicopter*

TO THE LOGGERS clearcutting old-growth timber on a small
bench halfway up the mountainside, the dark-gray Sikorsky helicopter seems no bigger or scarier than a dragonfly skimming above
the calm waters of Belize Inlet. But not for long. As the industrial aircraft lowers its load of logs into the marine boom ground, turns its
plastic bug-eyes in our direction, and flies hungrily back uphill for
more, it quickly assumes predatory, run-for-your life proportions. In
a matter of seconds it is upon us, bullying its way into the cutblock
with storm force, the heart-squeezing roar of its engines reverberating
off the hillsides, the wind from its rotor bending standing timber and
stripping away ground debris as easily as picket fences in a tornado.
And then it stops. Hovers. Directly overhead. Ravenous. Demanding.
Now!

175

Amid the chaos of flying branches, the trembling of the earth, the sense that something apocalyptic is happening, Kevin Delves responds to the call and offers himself up as a sacrifice. The hooker with Coulson Forest Products Ltd. stands in a patch of felled timber, hardhat cinched firmly under his chin, and reaches toward the belly of the beast. Grabbing the hook dangling from a sixty-metre long line — a steel conduit that can ripple with enough static electricity to straighten hair — he attaches it to a nine-metre choker cable wrapped around four logs. Then he gets the hell out of there, making his way with tight-rope accuracy across a slippery tangle of logs and slash until he is free of the deadly load.

Pilot Gary Wiltrout cranes his neck out the cockpit's bubble window, watches Delves skip away to safety, and puts his shoulder into it, hoisting up a load with a weight equivalent to that of three Volkswagens. Then he carves a neat arc above the clearcut and roars back downslope, keeping one eye on the logs trailing below him, the other on the unforgiving mountainous terrain looming ahead. As the helicopter reaches the Belize Inlet boom site, the pilot activates the cable-release switch and watches the payload plunge neatly into the Pacific Ocean, to await towing to the mills of Vancouver.

On cue, chaser Bob DeBourcier motors over in his aluminum skiff to retrieve the float-equipped choker cable and return it to the wood dock, identified by a small blue building with red lettering, "The Happy Shack." There the cable is stacked with others into bundles of fifteen to be flown back up the mountainside to the loggers. That's assuming everything goes well. Standing in his cleated boots, wearing a hardhat, life preserver, and ear protectors, DeBourcier, the son of a water bomber pilot, recalls the time a pilot dropped his load too high and was positioned too close. One of the logs plunged below the surface, rocketed back up at an angle with missile force, and knocked his skiff over, flipping DeBourcier into the water. "Just a freak," he says of the hazards endured for twenty dollars an hour. "But it happens once in a while."

When conditions are just right — the helicopter doesn't break down, the moody weather of British Columbia's mid-coast cooperates, and the entire logging crew operates with timepiece precision — Wiltrout and co-pilot Greg Root can make a return trip about every three minutes throughout their grueling twelve-hour shift. "You could compare us to the Wild West gunfighter," offers Wiltrout, a fifty-year-old Idahoan who flew helicopters in Vietnam. "I have to accept that I'm not as good as I once was and that I'm not smart enough to quit."

The analogy is close to the mark. British Columbia is experiencing a new frontier boom as North America's hot spot for heli-logging, the fastest-growing sector in a provincial forest industry worth up to $16.5 billion a year. Although helicopters have been used in logging operations in North America since 1957 — a decade after they first went into commercial use — their presence in British Columbia is much more recent, beginning with a small operation in the Strait of Georgia in 1975. Three years later, Whonnock Industries launched a heli-logging subsidiary that became Helifor, one of the largest such operations in the province. From a modest harvest of 200,000 cubic metres of timber per year and one machine before 1992, the company increased its annual take to 950,000 cubic metres with four machines by 1997.

Consistent with Helifor's growth, the number of forest companies in British Columbia expanding into heli-logging has also ballooned, to fifteen. Helifor attributes the expansion to heli-logging's "speed, efficiency, and sensitivity to the environment." But it would be closer to the truth to say that heli-logging is able to play a unique role that conventional logging cannot, and that as environmental concerns about logging grow and the accessible stands of old-growth timber shrink, more and more companies are turning to helicopters by default, despite their high operating costs. For example, a twenty-year-old Sikorsky S-61 helicopter costs an estimated $3 million, sucks up 725 litres of fuel an hour, and requires two $150-an-hour pilots plus a full-time maintenance crew. The machine has a thousand components, each with a unique life span that is inevitably cut in half by the daily rigors of heli-logging. The Sikorsky's main rotor blade is worth US$100,000 and gets replaced every 9,400 hours, after barely a year's work. As such, heli-logging is affordable only where cheaper conventional methods are impractical or where geographic or environmental conditions dictate a less intrusive form of logging. Belize Inlet is one such place, a fabulous fjord that is one kilometre wide, 325 metres deep, and slices fifty kilometres into the central coast. Numbingly cold glacial creeks erupt with volcanic force down steep, scoured slopes, evidence of the heavy rainfall that dominates this region and fuels the growth of red and yellow cedar, western hemlock, and amabilis fir. These forests represent priceless ancient ecosystems to environmentalists locked in a campaign to save the best, last stands of old growth, but they are lucrative timber sources to an industry whose economic back is up against the wall.

Operating a logging camp 350 kilometres by air northwest of Vancouver is no easy task. To access cutblocks in these remote areas with maximum speed and minimum damage to the landscape, Coulson Forest Products has converted an oceangoing ship, the MV *Coulson Marine One*, into a floating heli-landing pad and logging camp. When I arrive aboard a daily floatplane flight from Port Hardy, a timber and fishing community on northern Vancouver Island, the ship is tied up along the south side of the inlet beside a veiled waterfall that splashes down an old clearcut logging site. The terrain is unforgiving, best admired from a distance as it rises steeply from the water's edge, and offers little hope of refuge for pleasure craft in distress or even a handhold for the adventurous hiker.

The ship's second engineer, Dan Newman, is waiting to take me on a quick tour of the vessel, which he explains is equipped with bunks for up to fifty workers, a well-stocked mess hall, an exercise area with weights and ping-pong table, an incinerator for burning garbage, a sewage-treatment plant, and a desalination plant capable of making sea water potable at the rate of six litres a minute. Leading the way through a labyrinth of halls and stairwells to the ship's main deck, he looks across the inlet to the heli-loggers at work and concludes that a typical logging operation with gravel roads winding up the hillside to the clearcuts would be impossible in Belize Inlet. "You couldn't do a conventional show here because it's so steep. A switchback road would really screw it up."

Environmental concerns reflected in tighter roadbuilding restrictions in British Columbia's 1995 Forest Practices Code have contributed to the rapid growth of heli-logging. Unlike conventional logging, heli-logging requires neither road construction nor the use of a grapple yarder — a sort of industrial clothesline with a powerful claw used to drag logs up from the clearcut to the loading area. As a result, there is less damage to the ground and less risk of soil or gravel sloughing down steep slopes or silting up fish streams in heavy rains.

Heli-logging is also suited to smaller, irregular cutblocks, where boundaries follow the contours of the landscape rather than the crude straight lines of a traditional clearcut. In theory, these designer clearcuts make for a more pleasing viewscape, the curves and flowing lines following the terrain's natural features. But the distinction is lost on me. The larger issue with clearcuts is not just the way they look, but their effect on the ecology of the rainforest. Contoured clearcuts seem a desperate attempt by forestry to camouflage an unpalatable concept; they are little more than the snake oil of modern pitchmen.

For timber managers, however, heli-logging provides a valuable option, a way to hold environmental critics at bay while keeping the industry busy and productive. As explained by Jack Dryburgh, manager of the Port McNeill forest district, which includes a vast area of northern Vancouver Island and the mainland coast, the Belize Inlet site ideally meets the criteria for such an operation. The site is remote and difficult to access, with no existing network of logging roads, and offers a relatively small amount of wood, four cutblocks totaling just 105 acres. From an esthetic point of view, the clearcuts are also invisible to anyone traveling the inlet, since cutting takes place at an elevation of 1,000 to 1,500 feet, near Lost Hat Lake. "Environmentally, it's a real plus," Dryburgh insists. "There are benefits all around."

Conservationists aren't nearly so convinced. They have launched an international campaign to preserve the Great Bear Rainforest, as they call the province's central coast, stretching more than 600 kilometres from the upper Squamish River, north of Vancouver, towards the Alaska Panhandle. The lead group pushing for this broad-brushed protection, the Raincoast Conservation Society, views heli-logging as an activity that has evaded public scrutiny for too long. The society points out that while the public perceives helicopters as engaging in selective logging, a method to which they are well suited, the reality is quite different: heli-loggers engage in the same clearcutting practices in British Columbia as do conventional loggers.

By logging at higher levels, the industry also reduces the amount of denning habitat for grizzlies, which like to snuggle into the massive root cavities of old-growth trees at a snowy elevation of 3,000 feet to avoid getting rained out prematurely in a warm spell. And heli-logging is supported by public subsidies as it targets the best remaining old-growth forests on steep, slide-prone slopes. "This invasion is going on much more quickly than people realize," argues Raincoast founder Peter McAllister, predicting that it's only a matter of time before heli-logging companies, too, are hit by anti-logging protests. "Despite the ecological values of these last remnant valleys, they've been able to get immediate and easy access through heavy subsidies."

McAllister is not alone in his fears. Greenpeace Canada, which in 1997 committed $150,000 of its approximately $6 million annual budget to fight old-growth clearcutting in British Columbia, complains that only 6 percent of the province's ancient and biologically diverse temperate rainforests are protected. "We have a real concern," says Tamara Stark, the organization's Vancouver-based forest campaigner. "They are getting into the last vestiges of old growth, logging unstable slopes where there should be no logging at all."

In areas where heli-logging is deemed to be the most suitable method of harvesting, the British Columbia forests ministry lowers the stumpage or royalty rates charged for extracting timber from Crown lands to compensate the companies for their additional costs. In the Vancouver forest region, encompassing most of the British Columbia coast, heli-logging operators in 1996 were charged an average stumpage of $10.64 per cubic metre — in some cases, getting the wood pretty much for free — compared with an industry average of $26.93.

While Dryburgh agrees that heli-logging has facilitated clearcutting in areas that would otherwise be off limits, he dismisses the notion that the industry has created soil stability problems on steep terrain. At Belize Inlet, at least, he seems to be right. You could find logging on steeper slopes pretty much anywhere on the lower coast or on Vancouver Island. And the absence of a logging road — one of the most devastating impacts of a clearcutting operation — is an undeniable plus. However, Dryburgh also argues that the current boom in heli-logging will be short-lived. He predicts that the industry will level off or decline within fifteen years as the number of remote, high-elevation, old-growth stands lessens and more accessible second-growth stands are opened for cutting. Of course, that is precisely why environmentalists see the urgency in protecting these ancient coastal stands, before industry makes preservation a lost issue.

Heli-logging in the Port McNeill district alone was expected to grow by 20 percent through 1999, exceeding 500,000 cubic metres of timber annually, or 10 percent of the district's total harvest. In contrast to Dryburgh's prediction, some industry observers predict the coastal figure will go as high as 40 percent in the next decade as the number of heli-logging companies grows. "The boom isn't over," insists Helifor general manager Gary Laidlaw. "There's a lot of inaccessible stands that we really haven't touched yet. And there's a lot of companies that haven't started helicopter logging. They'll eventually have to get into it in a big way."

In the meantime, the environmental benefits attributed to heli-logging must be weighed not just against environmentalists' complaints but against the inherent hazards of the job. Heli-logging in British Columbia in 1996 resulted in 224 Workers' Compensation Board disability claims, costing $2.9 million in benefits and 9,424 lost working days — making it easily the most dangerous occupational sector in the provincial workforce.

Part of the problem is that the relatively expensive nature of heli-logging forces a race against time from the moment the helicopter is fired up. "It's almost like a sport," confirms Coulson heli-logging manager Brian Bell. "Our ground crews need timing and balance, but they must also be able to think fast and be versatile. No wasted movement — that's the key." Only hours before my arrival, hooker Eddie Murphy took a hit to his abdomen from a hook and had to be airlifted back to base camp for treatment. "The long line couldn't have jumped more than five feet in the wind," he recalls, still groggy from the effect of painkillers. "But it fucking hit me." Murphy is quick to acknowledge that heli-logging crews have higher production levels than conventional crews, but he is also the first to admit there is a price to be paid. "Shit happens. You get $25 an hour — danger pay."

A young man's game on the ground, heli-logging is squeezing out older forest workers who have not kept themselves fit. The maneuverability of heli-logging, requiring loggers to relocate to a dozen or more sites per year, can also prove to be an unacceptable inconvenience to the older family man. Don Smith spent fifteen years at conventional logging before getting into heli-logging at age thirty-five. In 1996, after just five years at the job, his legs and back gave out, and he quit to start his own company, International Heli-logging Training Institute, in Courtenay, on Vancouver Island. Now he calls the shots, charging almost $4,000 for a five-and-a-half-week ground-crew training course. The average age of his first students was about twenty-three; the oldest was forty-six. Only the fittest middle-aged loggers are up to the task, which can preclude workers who have spent years as immobile heavy-equipment operators. "Yeah, I guess resentment is a good word," Smith says of the older woodworkers' attitude. "If someone is used to sitting in a machine, they won't have the endurance."

For helicopter flight crews, the dangers are different but no less real. The Transportation Safety Board of Canada recorded sixteen heli-logging accidents throughout British Columbia in the three-year period ending April 1997. Helicopters, including smaller support craft such as the popular Bell 206 and Bell 222, used for transporting crew and equipment from camp to logging site, go down for all kinds of reasons. Some crash while landing on makeshift landing pads in clearcuts. Others suffer mechanical failure from the long hours of heavy work. Logs can shift position during flight and make the aircraft oscillate. Violent winds can suck a slow-moving helicopter into the ground before the crew can react. There is the ever-present risk of snagging the long line or the logs on standing timber or on the ground. And the tremendous stress on the machines means there is always a risk of engine failure. In one tragic case involving a Coulson operation at Stave Lake in the Fraser Valley east of Vancouver, an unloaded Sikorsky experienced mechanical problems and crashed into a stand of trees, killing the co-pilot and seriously injuring the pilot.

Federal regulations for aerial work, adopted in 1996, prohibit heli-logging pilots from flying more than 150 hours per month, 300 hours in a three-month period or 1,200 hours a year. Pilots cannot be on duty more than fourteen hours a day and must be allowed eight hours of rest every night. Bill Yearwood, Transport Canada's systems safety manager in Vancouver, has flown helicopters for most of his working life. He spent several years in the heli-logging industry and is confident the regulations provide a reasonable level of safety in an industry that often defies description. "It's a strange arm of aviation, a bastardized son of both aviation and logging. At the same time, it's an efficient means of moving trees."

In remote camps, where pilots work, eat, and sleep for two weeks, then fly home for two weeks, the flight regulations work well. But where logging occurs close to communities, the system can break down if pilots choose to engage in social activities that encroach on sleep time. "When you go into town, guys might want to stay out and go to the pub or a movie. The eight hours is hard to police."

At the Coulson operation, pilot and co-pilot switch seats every seventy minutes when the helicopter lands for refueling and a mechanical check. It is an important break from a job that never seems to let up, never allows the crew one moment of mental relaxation, never lets them forget their own safety or the vulnerability of the ground crew. The process of picking up and dropping off the logs is tantamount to a 747 pilot spending a twelve-hour shift strictly on take-offs and landings. "This can be a very unforgiving deal," Wiltrout confirms during a break. "You can't become complacent."

To make matters worse, the machines are hot in summer and cold in winter, when the rotor can actually produce its own fog bank, and they are always loud and rumbling with vibration. When something does go seriously wrong — a log becomes jammed, say, or the long line release switch fails — crew members entrust their lives to each other. "Have a conversation in a bar and people will say, 'It must be a dangerous job,'" adds Root, who compares heli-logging to making love — on some days you're simply better than on others. "But it can't be. The job has so many variables and split-second decisions. You have to make it as smooth and safe as possible. If you are stressed out, it's time to quit, or someone will get hurt." Then he considers his words carefully and adds with a smile, "It's like doing aerobatics ten hours a day. If it ever gets boring, you should have your head examined."

Despite the associated dangers, workers continue to be attracted to the industry for the good pay, yes, and for the singular challenges. "You must be confident," confirms Delves, a thirteen-year logger, the last five in the fast-growing helicopter sector. "One false step and you lose it." Hookers poised beneath the fury of the Sikorsky, fighting off bark and branches kicked up in the rotor wash, savor the fact that they must not only be fleet of foot but adept at mentally calculating the size and number of felled logs to match the Sikorsky's abilities. Each load contains anywhere from one to five logs, depending on the size and species of tree.

The intricacy of the job is summarized in a manual that hookers must commit to memory: for example, a load of 3,375 kilograms would require a western red cedar log 12.3 metres in length with a 71-centimetre-diameter top. Imagine trying to estimate that in a tunnel of wind and rain with a guillotine whirling overhead. "This one was too heavy for the helicopter to lift," says Delves, straining to wrap the choker cable around a grand-daddy red cedar. "I had to split it in half with the saw." For a flight crew poised to take off over a rock cliff, it can indeed be a leap of faith, knowing full well that an excessive load can drag them to their death.

Leaving Delves to his job, I struggle up, over, and through a horrific tangle of clearcut slash to reach an elite member of the logging
crew, Ken Wiley, a faller who earns up to $400 for a six-and-a-half-
hour day. The short but exhausting journey gives me a new-found
appreciation for the challenge and danger associated with cutting
timber under such conditions. Wiley informs me that conventional
logging requires less "manufacturing" than heli-logging, a reference to
the trimming off of limbs and the bucking of the logs into bite-sized
chunks for the aircraft. Still, during a typical shift he is capable of cutting down enough timber to fill two and a half logging trucks. Heli-
logging makes him feel good about minimizing the potential for slope
damage in the years to come as new growth returns to shore up the
slopes. In the final analysis, however, it's just another ugly clearcut.
Slicing his chainsaw through an old-growth cedar, wood chips flying
out like spray from a jet boat, the eleven-year logging veteran looks
down at the knot of debris and concedes matter-of-factly: "I'm the
guy who starts it. It's not much to look at except destruction."

Still, logging is not an entirely brutish affair. Wiley wipes his brow
and recalls the time he spotted a woodpecker working its way down a
snag in search of wood bugs. When it came to a neat round hole in
the log, a small but annoyed owl popped out, grabbed the woodpecker in a death grip with its talons, and wrestled it to the ground.
Watching the drama unfold from a distance, Wiley downed his tools,
sprinted over, and broke up the fight. "The owl was just a weenie little thing, but he had that woodpecker. Fuck, they're meat eaters!"

Diminutive figures toiling on a vast wilderness landscape, these
woodworkers say that despite what environmentalists tell you, heli-
logging is a sure bet, a progressive industry with a bright future. In the
real world of compromise, the intimidating thump of a rotor blade
might be the most benign offering possible from industrial forestry.
One thing's certain: some matters are beyond the control even of heli-

logging, its big powerful machines, and its army of well-trained, well-paid workers. The raw, unbridled forces of the central British Columbia coast remain one of them. By early afternoon, low clouds roll off the Pacific, spill across the mountaintops as softly as cotton balls, and tumble down into the valley bottoms. The rain pours down with monsoon force, heavy deliberate drops on an inky black ocean. Logging screeches to a halt. The hookers and the chasers are idled. The Sikorsky is grounded.

Pilot Wiltrout, like an athlete potentially deprived of a record season, laments the lost chance for just one more two-minute turn-around. "Any logging pilot is very competitive," he confirms, noting that in this high-pressure, high-volume world there are younger pilots with quicker reflexes waiting to take his job. "You always want just one more. You have to produce, and you have to figure the fastest way to do it. There is always going to be someone faster than you."

# CHAPTER 12

# The Salmon Forest

*Death and Rebirth
on Chichagof Island*

THE PATH TO understanding the relationship between the salmon and the rainforest begins with a crude trail leading from the back door of ecologist Mary Willson's research lab on the outskirts of Juneau, Alaska. Elsewhere in North America, scientists travel hours, even days, to conduct their field research. Not so for Willson. Her destination is a five-minute traipse through a second-growth forest of western hemlock and around boggy patches of skunk cabbage en route to a ditch-size creek that is habitat for coho salmon, Dolly Varden char, and cutthroat trout. Here, within earshot of passing tourist traffic on the Glacier Highway, Willson and her staff have distributed the carcasses of forty pink salmon — donations from a local fish shop — on the forest floor as far as thirty feet from the creek. The sides of the fish have been sliced open to simulate the natural swipe of a bear claw and to expose the flesh to a host of invertebrate invaders.

Just two hours into the experiment, the scene is already turning ugly, providing a glimpse into the dark world of a kingdom that may some day inherit the earth. Black flies are the first to arrive, depositing their eggs into the salmon's gaping mouths, a fertile home for writhing maggots. On top of them, parasitic wasps are busy laying their eggs, which will hatch and consume the maggots before they have a chance to develop. No less strange is a host of sexton beetles busy gnawing off pieces of salmon to be carted away and buried. The same beetle is also known to roll up dead mice and shrews, tucking the rodents' legs neatly underneath and carting them away as larders for their young. "They are really cool," Willson proclaims. "They belong to the genus Necrophorus, which tells it all. They carry the dead."

The victor is never clear in this process. A fox or raven could arrive at any moment to scavenge the salmon carcass and disrupt the insect free-for-all. But it doesn't really matter. The point of the exercise is to open our eyes to the importance of salmon to all levels of the food chain, especially salmon transferred by bears from their spawning beds to the riverbanks, where their decaying bodies benefit a host of species, including those in the rainforest itself. As Willson is finding, the interrelationship between logging and salmon may be as well documented as the link between smoking and cancer: clearcutting and road construction damage fish habitat by silting up the water and spawning gravels, removing the forest cover, and altering the water temperatures.

But research into the ways that an intact rainforest and all its associated flora and fauna depend on the salmon is only beginning. Nowhere is that relationship more dramatic than southeast Alaska, where more than 40 species of mammals and birds are known to feed on salmon during the freshwater phase of the fish's life cycle alone, either as eggs, juveniles, or spawning adults. Marauding gulls are quick to gouge out the eyes, the most easily scavenged part of a salmon before decomposition. Bears especially enjoy the skin, brain, and eggs — up to 3,000 sweet little ball-bearings can be consumed at a single gulp. Even shorebirds and dickie birds will nibble away at spawned-out salmon, as do Sitka black-tailed deer, presumably as a diet supplement. And, in the ultimate cycle of life, young fry emerging from their eggs are quick to cannibalize the putrefying bodies of their parents as their first food source in the free world.

But wildlife are more than simply opportunists showing up for a free meal. Some species' natural history has evolved around the seasonal arrival of spawning salmon. Bears with access to salmon have larger, healthier cubs than those that do not prey on the fish. Mink time their breeding cycle so that the birth of their young coincides with the return of the salmon — a high-protein source of food that helps females during the lactation period. And fledgling bald eagles leave their nests in southeast Alaska just as the massive pink salmon runs begin in August, a tactic that enhances their chances of survival at a time when they are least experienced at catching their own food.

Willson and her colleagues are among the first North American scientists to take the scenario one step further, looking at the ecological implications of bears removing spawning salmon from water and transplanting them onto land. Bears only eat part of their catch, so this transfer of resources from one ecosystem to another allows a host of predators and insects to feed on salmon that might otherwise be inaccessible to them. The rainforest also benefits by gaining a valuable source of fertilizer where it needs it most, in the riparian zone, that productive strip of vegetation along streambanks that moderates temperature; provides shelter and habitat for birds, animals, and insects; and shores up the soil as a defence against siltation. At the same time, a healthy and diverse buffer of trees provides a breeding ground for insects that are eventually washed into the creek in heavy rains or strong winds. "You'd be surprised what goes into the mouth of a salmon," Willson informs me. "Insects, needles, caterpillar larvae — they eat whatever hits the surface before someone else does. They can always spit it out or poop it out later."

A former professor of ecology at the University of Illinois at Champaign-Urbana, Willson has worked the past eight years at the United States Forestry Sciences Laboratory in Juneau. She is a feisty scientist with a deep, strong voice and an even deeper passion for nature. As an employee of the U.S. Forest Service, she is also something of a lone voice in the wilderness. She cannot hide her feelings, and I doubt that she tries very hard. Her scientific papers bristle with words and phrases that evoke passion for the wild world and sarcasm for the plight of public land management — "unconscionable," "much-vaunted sapience," "cripplingly limited," "draconian," and "mayhem."

These are not the utterings of a spineless bureaucrat unwilling to venture from beneath her safe rock. Willson is clearly a songbird at dawn — colorful, full-throated, and proudly perched for all to hear. She is also a scientist quick to show the ludicrousness of attempting to "manage" a rainforest and all its creatures when we still know so little about the ways each species interacts. There is little point in studying a single species, endangered or not, without first knowing how it relates to the diversity of life forms around it. And it is equally unrealistic to research predator-prey interactions — the cyclical link between the lynx and snowshoe hare is a classic example — while ignoring nature's mutually beneficial arrangements, of which flowering plants and pollinating bees are but one case.

Nor can we study a species without taking into account the potential for variations in populations. Consider the red crossbill, a colorful and nomadic bird whose existence is tied to the availability of conifer seeds. Different crossbills throughout western North America have evolved different beaks, specialized to extract seeds from specific trees — Douglas fir, western hemlock, lodgepole pine, ponderosa pine, Sitka spruce. It is indeed a small example — the strangely configured beak is all but impossible to spot on the finch-sized bird — but it clearly shows the dangers of making general assumptions based on a study of a single population.

As an ecologist always searching for evidence demonstrating the greater web of life, Willson recalls one particularly enlightening visit to Berners Bay, north of Juneau, traveling in early May by ocean kayak and Zodiac. Her objective was to study the ecological impact of spawning oolichans, an oily little fish pronounced "hooligans" by Alaskans. The fish once represented an important trading item for aboriginal people, especially on British Columbia's central coast. As the oolichan numbers began to swell in Berners Bay, Willson could almost hear the surge of approaching wildlife, as clear as the rumble of hooves on the Serengeti. The sky and land grew heavy under the weight of bird and marine life drawn to the sudden glut of food. The number of gulls went from a few hundred to 50,000 in just two days, the bald eagles from half a dozen to 1,000 in a week. About 400 Steller sea lions showed up to gorge on the feast, the females bulking up on fats to get them through the challenge of birthing and nursing their pups. Long after the masses had left, ravens continued to pick away at the leftovers, stashing bits and pieces of oolichan on tree limbs for the hard times ahead, risking having them rain down like croutons in the first strong wind.

Today, the more Willson studies the interconnectedness of life in the rainforest, the more she is mystified by our presumptuousness in making long-term decisions about logging, mining, fishing, hunting, and trapping when we have so little information on the way in which we are affecting the big picture. We wouldn't even know the big picture if we saw it. And what if the unthinkable happens? What if, through human mismanagement, the salmon stop coming? Fishermen portray the collapse of fish stocks and the specter of social assistance as cultural genocide. But what about all those other species that have evolved side-by-side with the salmon over the millennia? "You need to know what you're doing before you blunder out and do it," says Willson. "I'm not too popular for thinking that."

Three-quarters of southeast Alaska — a panhandle of land pressed up against the northwestern shoulder of British Columbia — is swaddled in 50,000 square miles of coastal temperate rainforest, predominantly Sitka spruce and western hemlock. It can be a depressingly soggy place, especially in fall, when the heavy rains begin and seem to never let up, forcing some residents out of state on holidays in hopes of arranging their return to coincide with the arrival of snow. Exactly how rainy it gets depends on where you live: at the south end of the panhandle, exposed to the moisture-laden Gulf of Alaska, the city of Ketchikan gets an annual average of 148 inches of precipitation; almost 400 miles to the north, protected from the worst rainclouds by glaciated mountains towering above 6,000 feet, the historic gold-rush community of Skagway enjoys less than three feet.

Equally prolific in its natural resources, the region is a giant in the fishing industry. British Columbians proudly refer to the 850-mile-long Fraser River — the centre of a long-standing fisheries dispute between Canada and the United States over its prized sockeye catch — as the continent's most important salmon producer. But when it comes to overall numbers, the Fraser's sockeye are minnows in southeast Alaska's vast, wriggling ocean. Between 1990 and 1995, the region generated an average annual catch of 66 million salmon — 79 percent of them pinks and 11 percent chums, the two least commercially valuable of the Pacific salmon species. The other 10 percent was a combination of coho, sockeye, and chinook.

Southeast Alaska's salmon runs are so vast and far-flung that numerous streams are too small to be counted, too small to even carry a name. But each stream may represent a distinct salmon run, filling its own ecological niche in the rainforest. It is to one such stream on remote Chichagof Island that Willson's research associate, Scott Gende, has agreed to take me on this warm August day. The trip is a ninety-minute voyage aboard the United States Forest Service aluminum skiff *Maybe Not*, west through Icy Strait, a cold but nutrient-rich waterway linking Glacier Bay National Park to Admiralty Island and Juneau.

My first impression is that Gende is out of his element at this latitude. With shoulder-length hair, an easy smile, and California good looks, he gives all the appearances of a Malibu surfer. But this is the Last Frontier, and you do what you can. In his spare time he paraglides off Juneau's Mount Roberts, riding the thermals for more than an hour before being brought back to earth by biological necessity — the simple need to take a pee. Or he climbs some of the state's 100,000 glaciers with his ropes and gear. In fact, Gende has just returned from a two-week trip to the Valdez icefields, during which he followed a trail of encrusted blood left by a previous climber seriously injured in an accident.

But those are not all his passions. Gende allows that his favorite halibut fishing hole is just off Couvercer Point, a convenient pit-stop about halfway to our destination. Quick to adapt science and technology to his personal pursuits, he thrusts a handheld Global Positioning System unit out the window of the skiff and calculates our estimated time of arrival based on our coordinates. "At our current speed of twenty-two knots, we'll be there in twelve minutes, fourteen seconds," he announces with smug satisfaction.

The site is marked by a dozen fishing craft, some of them charter operations, bobbing earnestly on the surface. The halibut being hauled up today are no bigger than dinner plates, but it is not unusual around these parts to reel in monsters weighing ninety pounds. When they get that big, the drill is to shoot them with a gun rather than bring their writhing bodies on board and risk breaking someone's leg.

Gende muscles his way into the crowd and attaches a herring to the end of a heavy jigging rig. Then he lowers the rig to the ocean bottom, raises it back up slightly, and begins to work the rod as we drift slowly eastward through the fleet. But all the technology at his disposal won't put a halibut on his hook. He tries several times, eventually hauling up his line only to find the herring bait chewed off. "Bastards," he curses. "I thought so."

No one gets entirely skunked during a day of boating in southeast Alaska. Mother Nature sees to that. As we motor away from the other vessels it becomes evident that more than human predators are attracted to the productive waters of Icy Strait. A group of humpback whales engage in ritualistic feeding, blowing a net of bubbles into a school of small fish from below to disorient them before rushing headlong for the kill. Summer migrants to southeast Alaska from their wintering grounds in the Hawaiian Islands, the humpbacks put on a dramatic show, black backs arching neatly in descent, tail flukes silhouetted against the blue horizon, and ghostly plumes of white spray suspended vertically above their vent holes. Inquisitive or ignorant boaters who violate the zone of safety put both the whales and themselves at risk. It is not uncommon in southeast Alaska for the operator of a small pleasure craft to be flipped into the ocean by a humpback innocently surfacing for air, a scene reminiscent of the genre of nineteenth-century paintings that show devilfish rising up with malicious deliberation to crush the New World whalers.

Elsewhere around us, three tan-colored Steller sea lions — a species mysteriously in decline in south-central Alaska and the Aleutian Islands but apparently holding its own in the southeast — huddle together on a navigational buoy. Four white-and-black Dall porpoises explode across the water surface in a blinding splash of white foam. And pretty much everywhere, coho salmon propel themselves into the air and land with a beaver-tail slap, a move that might help rid them of annoying sea lice.

Before long, Gende is heading for Salt Lake Bay in the farthest reaches of Port Frederick, a pale-blue tongue of water reaching so far inland that it virtually severs the northeast corner of Chichagof from the rest of the island. He leaves behind the last human settlement — Hoonah, the small Tlingit community — and steers his skiff toward an obscure stream known to researchers as Fecal Creek in recognition of the mounds of bear dung that befoul its banks. The creek is no more than twelve feet across, with just 300 yards of spawning gravel, but it provides habitat for up to 2,500 returning pink and chum salmon each year. And dinner for the likes of Binky, an affable young brown bear (the Alaskan term for a grizzly), who, despite his modest size, has managed to defend the creek mouth as his own. The daily presence of researchers prowling for salmon and rudely poking holes in Binky's turds causes him little concern. Within reasonable limits he is willing to share the spoils with humans, pose for photographs at close range, even haul out a salmon and join the research team for lunch on the sedgegrasses lining the estuary.

That team would include researcher Brian Marston, a transplanted Californian, now living in Juneau; Bobette Dickerson, a graduate student in fish science at the University of Washington in Seattle, who is basing her doctoral thesis on pink salmon spawning behavior; and two assistants, Dietrich Schmitt, also of Seattle, and Ray Vinkey of Missoula, Montana, who are both employed under Dickerson's research grant. Dickerson is the only native-born Alaskan among them.

She grew up and graduated from high school in Anchorage before moving to Reno, Nevada, for her college education. She embodies the characteristics of the Last Frontier — independent, gregarious, and completely at ease in the wilderness, even when she shouldn't be. Less than one year after her stepfather, a hunting guide-outfitter, was seriously mauled in a brown-bear attack on the Alaska Peninsula, Dickerson is nonchalant about the untamed rainforest, acting like it is a walk through an arboretum. She carries no gun or bear bell and disdains shouting to announce her presence, even in thick brush. "You don't make noise when you travel through the bush," she insists, believing it is better to die in a bear attack than rot away in old age like a spawned-out salmon. "You travel as quietly as possible."

I am not convinced. As we proceed upstream I carry a can of pepper spray in my right hipwader, just in case Binky — named after a polar bear who once inhabited the Anchorage zoo — is not the loveable furball he appears to be. His claws are already the size of small pitchforks, a reminder that a grizzly's appetite extends well beyond wild honey and tubers. The bumper of my pickup truck carries the Smokey mantra "Support Your Local Bear." But trust? That is another matter. I trust no bear, especially a boisterous teenager who has not yet learned the ways of the world, who has no fear of humans. Indeed, at a distance of thirty feet, Binky lets us know that there is a limit to his good nature. He takes several deliberate, pigeon-toed steps toward us. Dickerson immediately backs off and leads us up the streambank in a wide arc around him. "Back away," she instructs. "It's okay, Binky." Not one to hold a grudge, Binky quickly returns to fishing, bites into a pink salmon so hard it sprays a fountain of milt into the air, then carries it back into a thicket of devil's club to be eaten in private. "The first day out here was a bit scary," Dickerson concedes. "But he couldn't care less. He knows us, and he's never shown any threatening behavior."

Judging by the number of carcasses on the creek banks, it is evident the chum run has peaked — enough putrid carcasses lie here to turn a person off canned salmon for life — and the pinks are just starting to build. But there is still enough overlap to make separating the two species a laborious, painstaking process. Researchers set a beach seine net at the mouth of the creek each afternoon — throwing out the chums and tagging the pinks so they can be studied in the coming weeks. Come spawning time, the chum assume a demonic aspect, sprouting scimitar teeth that help them fight for their place in the spawning beds. Fishermen call them dogs. No one can say which came first, the razor-sharp teeth to penetrate the chum's thick skin, or the skin as armor against the teeth. All researchers know for sure is that extracting a chum from a tangled seine net is far less appealing than a walk through a darkened forest crawling with bears. It is a hard-earned art that required at least one researcher to be transported off-site for medical treatment of a badly infected finger. "They are evil and nasty," Dickerson says with unscientific dislike. Pink salmon, also known as "humpies" for the pronounced bump that develops on the male's back during spawning, are a gentler breed. Their biological clock also makes them a convenient research subject: the pink is the only species of Pacific salmon that returns to spawn in two years, half the time required to study a chum.

Dickerson wades purposefully upstream, stopping whenever she spots a marked fish — identified by a two-letter tag pinned below its dorsal fin — and takes note of the location, vegetation type, water depth and velocity, size of spawning gravel, and, of course, the company it keeps. "HP used to be in a good spot with three females," Dickerson says, staring into the waters with her binoculars. "Now he's by himself." Upon reaching a stretch of the creek rife with chaos — fighting, mauling, biting — Dickerson is moved to remark, "This is a big pool of males. They haven't established a hierarchy yet."

Researchers believe female pink salmon are attracted to males with big humps. You don't need a Ph.D. to figure that one out. But it's really not that simple, she explains. In shallow spawning channels such as Fecal Creek, the humps protrude well above the water surface and become moving targets for brown bears. What are the genetic tradeoffs for the pink salmon, and how have they evolved to meet the challenges specific to this little creek? These are the mysteries Dickerson is keen to resolve as she explores the secret sex life of the humpie.

As any human bar scene habitué can attest, the only thing predictable about spawning behavior is that when a female is ready, the males are certain to follow. But in the heat of the moment the salmon can become, well, a little confused, even indiscriminate. "We've had male chum courting female pinks, and male pinks courting female chum," Dickerson confides. And in a desperate tactic best left to fish, smaller males have been known to pretend they are females, thereby avoiding battles with the larger males and allowing them to sneak in and fertilize a female's eggs right under a competitor's hump.

Despite walking this route repeatedly during her two-month summer research period, Dickerson refuses to hack out a trail that would make the jaunt easier on herself. She's afraid it might alter the bears' feeding behavior. Instead she wades through the creek, struggles up and over fallen logs, and shoehorns her way through thick scrub. As we continue upstream, the immediate effect of the rainforest on the salmon is clear: fallen logs provide not just relief from the sun, but the only hope of escape from marauding bears. At one corner of the creek the fish are able to secret themselves a full six feet into the root cavity of an ancient Sitka spruce. "There was a male here for four days, then he just disappeared," she remarks. "He must have been dragged out and munched."

Halfway up the creek, we leave behind Binky's fishing territory and enter the domain of a female bear with three newborn cubs.

Despite the renowned aggressiveness of a mother brown bear, this one maintains a wary truce with humans. Dickerson has seen the female several times this summer under a full range of conditions — lounging lazily on the mud bank, quietly nursing, and in full battle with another bear threatening her cubs. "When she chased him through the woods, it was like heavy machinery. I thought, 'It's all over.'"

Dickerson finds a mossy log over the creek and curls up to conduct her research. Asked why she got into fish science, she explains that the most beautiful places on earth are next to streams and lakes. By studying fish, she is assured of always being around them. But that is the romantic image. Southeast Alaska can be a wet and miserable place for research; in fact, my arrival heralded the first few days of sunny summer weather. "Everything we owned was wet," she confirms. "If we'd been in tents, we'd've been miserable."

The research base camp is a simple but comfortable wood-frame shack on a floating platform a short swim from shore. There are half a dozen rooms — two for storage, two equipped with bunks for sleeping, a bathroom, and a mess-hall-cum-work-area complete with a woodstove for drying clothes and a propane stove for cooking. A drawing on the wall depicts a raincloud and beside it the sun, next to the comforting words "Prozac Can Help." The camp provides distance from the brown bears that patrol the shoreline for marine life at low tide and, equally important, from the mice that inevitably invade a land-based camp. Far from the scenic viewscape displayed to passengers on Alaskan cruise ships, this landscape is anything but pristine. As part of the timber supply area within the Tongass National Forest, the surrounding forest is pockmarked with clearcuts. One patch directly across from camp opened up the forest to a fierce winter wind that blew down a sizeable patch of good timber and plugged a small stream.

The cabin is located in a murky little inlet, poorly flushed by the tidal currents. Bits of foam, kelp, and seaweed float by on the water surface and raft together into unsightly slicks alongside the ropes used to tether the camp to shore. Yet the place is abuzz with life: hundreds of circling Bonaparte and mew gulls, pink salmon cannonading across the water surface, half a dozen river otters squatting under the camp platform, a pair of mink playing on the shoreline, and a sea lion ploughing noisily through the water with flared nostrils.

Given the good weather, I decide to forgo the comfy but crowded bunkhouse and instead set up tent on the perimeter boardwalk. The smell of baited crab traps provides an authentic touch, and the dark, seamless sky is an ethereal blanket of contentment. Rising in the middle of the night to relieve myself, I am surprised to find that I am creating my own celestial entertainment — minute, bioluminescent zooplankton spark their way across the water surface like shooting stars.

The next morning it is back to Fecal Creek for another day's work, this time with Gende and Marston, researchers who leave nothing to chance, carrying a 12-gauge shotgun for protection. Our job is to scour the riparian zone for salmon deposited by Binky and any other bears, document the sex and species of the fish, the distance they are found from the creek bank, and evidence of predation or decomposition. Any lingering romantic notion about salmon-and-rainforest research is quickly put to rest by the routine of the work. "Male, chum, belly," Gende shouts to Marston, who scribbles down the information. "Pretty maggot-ridden." Dark pancakes of bear dung are dissected for evidence of berries of devil's club, salmonberry, blueberry, and elderberry, which suggests that a healthy diet is a diversified one. A bear's digestive system is notoriously inefficient, sometimes passing whole berries through its system untouched.

Fish samples will be sent to Seattle for tests of lipid composition, including nitrogen, magnesium, calcium, and phosphorus, to help determine exactly what the salmon provides the bears in nutrition and the rainforest in fertilizer. So will the parts left behind by the bear — the spinach and broccoli of the salmon world, you might say — intestines, testes, gills, even the flesh to a certain extent. The results will help to reveal how the plants benefit comparatively from a salmon passed through the gut of an animal and one allowed to rot away on the forest floor. "It's a kind of a bang-for-your buck thing," Gende explains.

When the three of us reach the limits of the spawning habitat, we double back along the middle of the creek and look for in-stream information. My job is to count the number of dead fish, taking special note of those showing evidence of bear predation. It is a gruesome assignment. Skin peeled back here. A head ripped off there. A neck slashed. A belly chewed in half. A hump — ouch! — bitten right off. The results are surprising: 186 salmon with evidence of bear predation, compared with 57 — less than one-third — showing a natural death. There is no way of knowing how many of the 186 were chewed up after spawning. But the huge number, combined with the fact that bears prefer live catches, hints at a potential impact on salmon populations. One Alaskan study determined that black bears were responsible for killing 8 percent of the female spawners in a stream. Although the results vary widely, depending on the size of the stream and the number of fish and bears, scientists argue that bears pose a relatively insignificant threat to fish stocks compared with the greater problems of overfishing and habitat destruction.

Indeed, it is the human potential for disrupting fish runs that poses a threat to the brown bears of Alaska. Having evolved over thousands of years on a diet rich in salmon, the isolated brown bears of Chichagof Island might not be able to survive without them. This might be a classic case of a big and powerful species that has eaten itself into an evolutionary corner.

Watching Binky catch yet another salmon and haul it onto the tidal flats for lunch, I consider the precariousness of his claim to this stretch of spawning stream. The creek is too small to warrant recognition by state fish managers or by Binky's human competitors — the massive commercial fishing fleet, positioned out at sea. If the salmon stop coming, what are Binky's chances of securing new spawning territory, one not already guarded by bigger and more powerful bears?

There are immediate considerations, too, for Binky. No wildlife research is completely benign. Eight pink salmon died this afternoon when they were placed in a solution designed to immobilize them for tagging. Normally after their release the fish lie on the creek bottom, punch-drunk for a couple of minutes, before groggily drifting on their way. These ones took too strong a dose, went to sleep, and never woke up again, never got the chance to run the gauntlet of swatting, salivating bears.

Does Binky risk a similar fate? With hunting season beginning in just a month, his laissez-faire attitude is cause for concern. For the young bear's own good, researchers talk of instilling some fright into him on their last day with a few well-placed shotgun blasts into the air. But at this late stage, it might not be enough to counteract a season of familiarity with humans.

For the salmon, however, there is no hope of cheating fate this day. Theirs seems a violent, ugly end, even in its most natural form — biting and struggling their way to a successful spawn, only to watch themselves rot away in a slow, downward spiral. Yet even under these chaotic circumstances, the salmon continue to play their nourishing role in an act of symbiosis that affirms the very foundation and lifeblood of the coastal rainforest.

# Epilogue

WILDLIFE CAN BE frustratingly elusive in the temperate rainforest. Secretive and often nocturnal by nature, animals are quick to melt into the diffused lighting or hide among pockets of thick, knotted understorey. Yet the sighting of a wild creature in its natural environment can leave a stronger impression on the human spirit than any single tree or even swath of forest. Animals serve to personalize the experience and complete the picture, assuring us that the wilderness is still alive — for now at least — and not some glorified terrarium.

During my research into this book, one such experience stands out. It occurred on a summer's day while I was returning from a short hike to Fragrance Lake in Washington's Larrabee State Park. It was a simple, satisfying moment. Warm shafts of light filtered through the luxurious canopy, drying out the last droplets of dew still hanging heavy on the spider webs beside the trail. There were no biologists to lead the way and no expectations other than the sweet, steamy fragrance of a Douglas fir forest.

Midway along the hike, and for no particular reason, I looked to my left in a nonchalant sweep of the forest. And that is when I caught the eye of one of the rarest of rainforest dwellers, an endangered species that has done more than any other creature to galvanize debate in the land-use battle over the last ancient forests of the Pacific Northwest. It was a northern spotted owl.

Naturally I was excited at having found the rainforest's ultimate poster child, a species so fragile it is represented by fewer than 100 pairs in my home province of British Columbia. And to see one so close. It sat on a stump just three feet off the ground and thirty feet from the trail, a reflection perhaps of camouflage confidence — with its soft brown feathers and flecked white chest, the owl looked as unremarkable as a patch of bark.

But my enthusiasm was tempered by the bird's repose, its slightly bowed head and listless stare. At the risk of sounding maudlin or stooping to anthropomorphism, I must say it was a sad-looking creature, possessing none of the wild-eyed inquisitiveness, animation, or even smugness that I have come to associate with owls. Sure, maybe it was just a case of mid-day drowsiness. But, I swear, this bird gave all the appearances of carrying the weight of a species on its shoulders — an impression confirmed minutes later when I went for my camera, only to find the owl vanished when I returned.

Today, I cannot help but think of that experience when I consider the plight of the temperate rainforest. With the research for my book under my belt, there is much I now know about this shrinking landscape, but still much more that I cannot even begin to comprehend. What I do know is that as a society we have treated the rainforest badly over the past century — taken too much, understood too little, allowed self-interest to prevail time and again over caution.

Still, as we enter the next millennium, I remain hopeful that our long-held attitudes have begun to change. People appreciate that the value of an ancient evergreen forest extends far beyond stumpage fees and two-by-fours. And somewhere along the way, Paul Bunyan stopped being a folk hero and logger shows lost their luster. One faller from Prince George, in central British Columbia, confided to me not long ago that as someone who clearcuts the forest and hunts black bears for recreation, he fears that society has turned his son against him, robbed him of the pride a child should have in his father. To that man I would say that I have never heard an environmentalist seriously call for an end to all logging or a logger espouse the cutting of every last tree. Somewhere in the darkness of misunderstanding and ignorance that exists between society's polarized views lies the salvation of the rainforest and the survival of all species, even those as rare as the northern spotted owl.

# Index